May 13, 2009

Dear readers,

I wish you many
golden afternoons full
of good stories.

Happy reading,
Angelica Shirley Carpenter

Lewis Carroll

LEWIS CARROLL'S ENGLAND

LAKE DISTRICT

Warrington

Croft-on-Tees —

Whitby

•Coniston

Richmond

NORTH YORKSHIRE

• Daresbury

CHESHIRE

ENGLAND

• Rugby

Oxford

London

Thames River

Guildford •

Dover

Eastbourne

Brighton

Sandown

Freshwater

ISLE OF WIGHT

A LERNER BIOGRAPHY

Lewis Carroll

Through the Looking Glass

Angelica Shirley Carpenter

Lerner Publications Company / Minneapolis

To Carey

Lerner Publications Company
A division of Lerner Publishing Group
241 First Avenue North
Minneapolis, MN 55401 U.S.A.

Website address: www.lernerbooks.com

Library of Congress Cataloging-in-Publication Data

Carpenter, Angelica Shirley.
    Lewis Carroll : through the looking glass / by Angelica Shirley Carpenter.
        p.   cm. — (Lerner biographies)
    Includes bibliographical references and index.
    Summary: A biography of the mathematician, teacher, photographer, and author who wrote "Alice's Adventures in Wonderland."
        ISBN: 0-8225-0073-6 (lib. bdg. : alk. paper)
    1. Carroll, Lewis, 1832–1898—Juvenile literature. 2. Authors, English—19th century—Biography—Juvenile literature.
    3. Children's stories—Authorship—Juvenile literature. 4. Authors, English. [1. Carroll, Lewis, 1832–1898.] I. Title.
    PR4612 .C37 2003
    828'.809—dc21   2002003266

Manufactured in the United States of America
1 2 3 4 5 6 – JR – 08 07 06 05 04 03

Contents

"She had never before seen a rabbit with either a waistcoat-pocket or a watch to take out of it." This sentence is from the beginning of Lewis Carroll's (Charles Dodgson's) Alice's Adventures in Wonderland. The illustration is by John Tenniel.

Chapter One

Down the Rabbit Hole

On a golden afternoon, July 4, 1862, five friends walked together, talking and laughing. They were two young men, tutors and clergymen at Oxford University in England, and three young sisters, daughters of the college dean. Their path led from the college of Christ Church, along a stream, down to the River Isis.

Charles Lutwidge Dodgson, aged thirty, was tall and thin, with curly brown hair. Like his friend Robinson Duckworth, he was dressed casually in a white flannel suit and a hard white straw hat, called a boater. Charles was carrying a picnic basket.

Lorina Liddell, aged thirteen, Alice, ten, and Edith, eight, wore white ruffled dresses, white lacy socks, black ankle-strap shoes, and large straw hats. Edith's hair was auburn; both her sisters had dark hair. Lorina and Edith had long curls, but Alice wore her hair short and straight, with a "fringe," or bangs.

At Folly Bridge, Charles selected a rowboat, carefully placing each guest and the basket for balance. Then Charles "rowed bow" in front, and Duckworth "rowed stroke" behind

*In Oxford the River
Thames is known as
the Isis. It is still
peaceful, as it was in
1862.*

him. The oars moved sleepily that day, Charles recalled later;
it was too hot to work very hard. Alice steered from the center by moving the tiller rope. Sometimes the girls rowed—
Charles was teaching them how.

The Isis wound past weeping willows, their branches
trailing in the water. Swans paddled out from the shade to
meet the boat, circling back when they realized they would
not be fed. Cows and horses stood motionless in the fields,
and a flock of brown geese slept on the riverbank. Later
Charles recalled "the cloudless blue above, the watery mirror
below. . . . The boat slowly wound its way up the stream under
the bright summer sky with its happy crew and its music of
voices and laughter."

Soon three eager faces turned toward Charles. "Tell us a story, please!" said the girls, and, as usual, he was happy to oblige.

He told them of a little girl named Alice, who fell down a rabbit hole. Landing underground, she soon found herself swimming in a salty pool with curious creatures: a Mouse, a Duck (for Duckworth), a Lory (for Lorina), an Eaglet (for Edith), and a Dodo (for Dodgson).

Charles told how Alice and the others swam to shore and gathered on the bank—"the birds with draggled feathers, the animals with their fur clinging close to them—all dripping wet, cross, and uncomfortable."

"At last the Mouse, who seemed to be a person of some authority among them, called out, 'Sit down, all of you, and listen to me! I'll soon make you dry enough!'" (Illustration by John Tenniel for Alice's Adventures in Wonderland)

The girls recognized in the story their last trip on the river. The party that day had included Charles's older sisters, Fanny and Elizabeth. It had been a serious trip, with no stories or singing, as the girls had been awed by the "old ladies." As they floated downstream a heavy rain had swamped the boat, soaking the women in their large hats, full petticoats, and long, heavy dresses.

Robinson Duckworth, who had been there too, was much amused by the tale. "Dodgson," he asked, "is this an extempore romance of yours?"

"Yes," Charles replied, "I'm inventing as we go along."

At Godstow, about three miles upriver, they stopped for a picnic in the fragrant shade of a new-made haystack. Charles offered cakes from his basket, and despite the heat, they built a fire and boiled water in a kettle for tea.

The story resumed as Alice met some unusual beings—live playing cards. They joined Alice in a strange croquet game, with ostriches for mallets and hedgehogs for balls.

When Charles tired, the sisters begged him to continue. Once, during an exciting part of the tale, he pretended to fall asleep, but they woke him and made him go on. After a while he stopped, saying, "And that's all till next time."

"Ah, but it is next time!" they exclaimed, and he told a little more. When the air cooled, and shadows grew longer, they floated back to Oxford, singing popular songs like "Twinkle, Twinkle, Little Star."

Later Charles and Duckworth walked the girls back to their house, the Christ Church Deanery, home of the college dean. As they said good night, the sisters thanked Charles, and Alice added a special request: "Oh, Mr. Dodgson, I wish you would write out Alice's Adventures for me!"

The book *Alice's Adventures in Wonderland,* published in

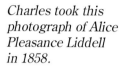
Charles took this photograph of Alice Pleasance Liddell in 1858.

1865, and its sequel, *Through the Looking-Glass and What Alice Found There,* are still read and loved. They were two of the first best-sellers published especially for children and two of the earliest books written purely to amuse (rather than to instruct) young readers. Known also for Charles's superb use of fantasy and language, they are acknowledged as two of the most important books in English and world literature.

When they were published, Charles Lutwidge Dodgson (whose middle name rhymes with "bridge," and whose surname is pronounced "Dodson"), used the pen name Lewis Carroll to guard his privacy and to protect his reputation as a serious scholar and tutor of mathematics.

In 1840 Charles's parents took him to the Warrington Exhibition, where each had a "likeness in paper" cut by Mr. Walker, Profilist. This silhouette, top, is the only known picture of Charles as a child.

Chapter Two

Chasing the Buffalo
1832–1851

Charles Lutwidge Dodgson was born January 27, 1832, in Daresbury, England. Named Charles after his father, he was his parents' third child and first son. His middle name, Lutwidge, was his mother's maiden name. Frances Jane Dodgson loved all her eleven children, but Charles was her favorite.

Charles's parents were first cousins. Many of his ancestors had been clergymen in the Anglican Church, or Church of England. Charles's father was Perpetual Curate of All Saints' Church in Daresbury, a village of two hundred people in Cheshire, a county in northern England. Though the position paid little, it included a farm and a large house, where Charles and nine of his brothers and sisters were born. The Dodgsons lived one and one-half miles from the village, on a road so quiet that the passing of a cart caused a stir of excitement.

Their house rang with children's laughter and babies' wailing. The family rose early, worked hard, and retired soon after sundown. Servants helped to run the household, but each Dodgson had a job to do.

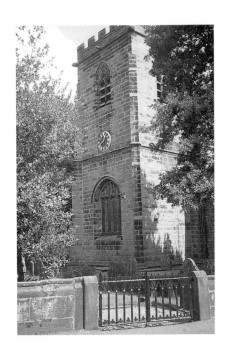

Inside the church tower at Daresbury is a plaque with an acrostic poem. The first letter of each line, read downward, together spell the name of the town. Charles would write many such poems.

The children resembled each other closely and most of them, including Charles, spoke with a hesitation. Later a friend described Charles's speech impediment: "It wasn't exactly a stammer, because there was no noise, he just opened his mouth. But there was a wait, a very nervous wait from everybody's point of view."

As the eldest son, Charles was expected to care for his siblings, even his two older sisters, Frances and Elizabeth. They and the younger children, Caroline, Mary, Skeffington, Wilfred, Louisa, Margaret, and Henrietta, loved to gather around Charles as he performed magic tricks or told stories, drawing pictures to accompany them. Sometimes Charles played with a friend, Thomas Vere Bayne, who was two years older. Vere's father, a clergyman, helped Mr. Dodgson with church services.

Charles's father was popular with his Daresbury parishioners. A respected scholar, Mr. Dodgson wrote many books on religious topics. The Bible, he believed, answered all problems and questions.

Mr. Dodgson taught his children at home and earned extra money by teaching neighbor children as well. In those days, boys studied mathematics and Latin while girls prepared for marriage by learning needlework, music, and painting. Although Mr. Dodgson encouraged his daughters to pursue academic subjects, only the boys prepared for college.

Mr. Dodgson expected his sons to attend Oxford University, as he had; to graduate with honors, as he had; and to become priests in the Church of England, as he had. A perfectionist in his own behavior, he expected no less from his children.

Charles was good at memorizing list after list—of kings and queens, dates of battles, countries, and such, as children did then. But he much preferred reading, and at age seven, he read *Pilgrim's Progress,* a long novel written for adults. In the humorless books of Charles's childhood, evil was always punished and virtue was always rewarded.

Like his father, Charles excelled at mathematics. At a very young age, he asked his father to explain logarithms, a mathematical device used to simplify computations. Mr. Dodgson replied that Charles was too young to understand.

"But, please, explain!" insisted Charles. To plead with his father was unusual. Charles lived in the Victorian era, named for Victoria, queen of England from 1837 to 1901. Victorian fathers were expected to be all-powerful in their families, and their word was seldom questioned. Mr. Dodgson was very strict, but loving.

He had a lively sense of humor too. Once, when planning a trip, Mr. Dodgson promised to buy Charles some tools. He wrote to his son:

> You may depend upon it I will not forget your commission. As soon as I get to Leeds I shall scream out in the middle of the street, *Ironmongers, Ironmongers.* Six hundred men will rush out of their shops in a moment—fly, fly, in all directions—ring the bells, call the constables, set the Town on fire. I WILL have a file and screw driver, and a ring, and if they are not brought directly, in forty seconds, I will leave nothing but one small cat alive in the whole town of Leeds, and I shall only leave that, because I am afraid I shall not have time to kill it. Then what a bawling and a tearing of hair there will be! Pigs and babies, camels and butterflies, rolling in the gutter together—old women rushing up the chimneys and cows after them—ducks hiding themselves in coffee-cups, and fat geese trying to squeeze themselves into pencil cases.

Sometimes Charles traveled with his father, on church business or to visit relatives in other towns. They went by horse and buggy, as the railroad had not yet reached their part of England.

In 1843, when Charles was eleven, his father was appointed rector in Croft-on-Tees, a resort town in Yorkshire, farther north in England. The new job included higher pay as well as improved living quarters. Before moving the family in, Mr. Dodgson had some changes made to the rectory, raising the ceiling over a bedroom and in the nursery above.

In 1950 workers renovating the house took up the nursery floor again and found a collection of items including a crochet hook, a letter from a child's alphabet, the lid of a doll's teapot, a little shoe, a penknife, a child's white glove, and a thimble. With them were three pieces of wood: two were inscribed June 18, 1843. Written on the third in Charles's hand were the words:

> And we'll wander through
> the wide world
> and chase the buffalo.

Someone, most likely Charles, had collected souvenirs from all the family and hidden them under a floorboard.

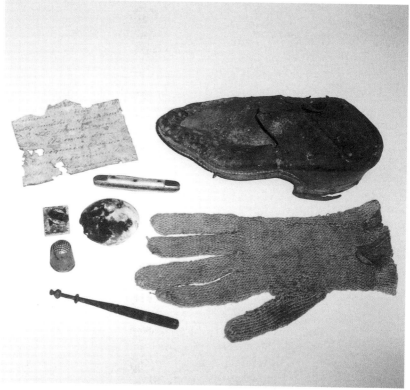

These are some of the items found under the Croft Rectory floorboard. The piece of wood with Charles's buffalo quotation has been stolen.

Mr. Dodgson described the rectory, which had a drawing room, dining room, study, sitting room, and:

> numerous bedrooms of all sorts and sizes...2 Kitchens, Servants' Hall, Butler's Pantry, House-keeper's Room, Scullery, Laundry, Brewhouse, Larder, Dairy, Coach House, Stabling for 7 Horses, Tithe Barn, Pigstyes, Henhouse—a large and excellent Kitchen Garden with...a small Flower garden separating the House from the Road.

The new rector was shocked to find that Croft had no school for the fifty or sixty children who lived there. Setting aside rectory land, he funded a school building using donations and gifts from his own family.

Charles's youngest brother, Edwin, was born at Croft in 1846, giving Charles a total of three brothers and seven sisters. He loved entertaining his siblings. When it snowed,

The Croft Rectory. Charles had a small bedroom on the top floor, in the back.

he stamped out a maze for them on the lawn. Other times, dressed as a magician in a brown wig and a long white nightshirt, he amazed the family with magic tricks.

The Dodgson children, and all of England, were fascinated by railways, which were spreading across the country. In the garden at Croft, Charles made a train from a wheelbarrow, a hand truck, and a barrel, and he wrote out rules: "All passengers when upset are requested to lie still until picked up—as it is requisite that at least 3 trains should go over them, to entitle them to the attention of the doctor and assistants."

Charles also developed a strong interest in the dramatic arts. Although educated people read plays at this time, many of them, including Mr. Dodgson, felt that theaters offered a low form of entertainment that was unsuitable for women, children, or clergymen. Charles, however, staged his own dramas at home. With help from the village carpenter, he built a puppet theater and fashioned marionettes. In his skillful hands, their movements seemed real as they performed plays he wrote himself.

At age twelve, Charles became the first child in his family to attend boarding school. Richmond School, just nine miles from Croft, was a small school for young boys. On August 1, 1844, Charles moved into the house of Headmaster James Tate II, rooming with another student.

Charles's first letter home, to his older sisters, said:

> The boys have played two tricks upon me . . . they first proposed to play at "King of the cobblers" and asked if I would be king, to which I agreed, then they made me sit down and sat (on the ground) in a circle round me and told me to say "Go to work" which I said, and they immediately began kicking and knocking me on

all sides. The next game they proposed was "Peter, the red lion," and they made a red mark on a tombstone (for we were playing in the church-yard) and one of the boys walked with his eyes shut, holding out his finger, trying to touch the mark . . . at last it was my turn, they told me to shut my eyes well, and the next moment I had my finger in the mouth of one of the boys, who had stood (I believe) *before* the tombstone with his mouth open. . . . The boys play me no tricks now.

At Richmond, Charles studied Christianity, Latin, Greek, literature, French, and mathematics. "He possesses . . . a very uncommon share of genius," wrote Headmaster Tate to Charles's parents. "You may fairly anticipate for him a bright career."

When Charles left Richmond in 1845, the new Croft school was completed. Mr. Dodgson, his wife, and his children, including Charles, all taught there occasionally.

Back at home, Charles created *Useful and Instructive Poetry,* the first of a series of family magazines he wrote and illustrated with his own pictures. He longed to become a good artist, but at age thirteen, his writing ability surpassed his drawing skills. One of his poems began this way:

> "SISTER, sister, go to bed!
> Go and rest your weary head."
> Thus the prudent brother said.
>
> "Do you want a battered hide,
> Or scratches to your face applied?"
> Thus his sister calm replied.

In February 1846, when Charles was fourteen, he "went up" to Rugby, one of England's most important "public" (Americans would say "private") schools. To reach the town

Rugby School. "I cannot say that I look back upon life at a Public School with any sensations of pleasure," wrote Charles later, "or that any earthly considerations would induce me to go through my three years again."

of Rugby, 150 miles south of Croft, Charles took the train. Rugby boys, trained to be Christians, gentlemen, and scholars, were expected someday to be leaders in Britain and its colonies around the world.

Rugby's curriculum was unusual for the time, offering "modern" subjects of French and history in addition to religion and the classics (Greek and Latin language and literature). Again Charles lived in the headmaster's house, a dormitory for eighty boys. These future gentlemen ate a poor diet of bread and meat with few vegetables. Even the youngest drank beer, served in pewter tankards. Given no way to wash their clothes, students grew grubbier as the term passed. Each boy received a pound of candles a week for light. At night rats skittered through the cold buildings.

Following a medieval tradition called "fagging," younger boys became servants, or "fags," to older students. The older boys controlled the sleeping rooms and, indeed, much of the school, with rules they invented. The younger boys' beds "in winter were denuded of blankets that the bigger ones might not feel cold." Little boys were "tossed" in blankets, sometimes leaving them black and blue. "If I could have been . . . secure from annoyance at night," Charles wrote later, "the hardships of the daily life would have been comparative trifles to bear."

Like the schoolmasters, older boys could punish younger students by assigning lines or "strokes"—formal beatings. "Handing" meant five or six raps on the back of the hand with a birch rod. Flogging "on the person" was for serious offenses such as smoking or "cheek" (disrespect).

These cruel practices were condoned by educators as necessary to prepare boys for leadership and upper-class life. Students who could not tolerate bullying were considered to be mentally and morally unfit. Contempt for discomfort may have helped graduates, who were expected to conquer the world. In Victorian times, the British Empire included colonies around the globe, captured and ruled by British military forces.

Charles avoided beatings, but his speech impediment made him a target for ridicule, as did his preference for studies over sports. But Charles was strong and fit, and he deplored bullying. As years passed, he became known as "a boy who knew well how to use his fists in defence of a righteous cause."

His high marks won him prizes, books of his own choosing. Charles selected biographies, histories, religious titles, and a Greek lexicon, or dictionary. For pleasure he read Shakespeare's plays and the novels of Charles Dickens.

Leaving Rugby in December 1849, seventeen-year-old Charles spent the next year happily at home, studying on his own and publishing *The Rectory Umbrella,* another family magazine. This publication, with caricatures of famous paintings, reflected Charles's growing interest in art. The subject was not taught in school, so Charles educated himself by reading and by visiting exhibits.

In 1850, at the age of eighteen, Charles matriculated, or enrolled, at Oxford University, at Christ Church, his father's old college. After passing an examination, Charles was fitted for a square black cap with a tassel and a long black gown, to be worn over his clothes. He received a copy of the statutes, rules for students that urged them "not to encourage the growth of curls," and "to refrain from football, fighting, and meeting to debate the Church or government of the University."

Swearing on his knees to observe the statutes, Charles signed his name to the Thirty-Nine Articles of religious faith of the Church of England (the only religion permitted at Oxford). Then he went back to Croft, as the University was overcrowded and no housing was available.

All the family enjoyed Charles's last six months at home. Mrs. Dodgson, especially, loved their life at Croft. She told her husband's aunt that "it really at times was 'alarming' to look round her & feel that she had not a wish unfulfilled."

On January 24, 1851, Charles "entered into residence" at Christ Church. A friend of his father, the Reverend Jacob Ley, had offered rooms in his apartment.

Two days later, Charles was called home.

Tom Tower, built in 1681, is the main entrance to Christ Church.
Architect Christopher Wren designed the tower to house the
seven-ton bell known as Great Tom.

Chapter Three

The City of Dreaming Spires

1851–1855

Charles had been called back to Croft to attend his mother's funeral. The news came as a terrible shock, for she had not been ill. Her death certificate listed "inflammation of the brain," possibly a stroke, as the cause of death. Aged forty-seven, she left ten children at home, the youngest, Edwin, only four years old.

Mrs. Dodgson's younger sister, Lucy Lutwidge, moved to Croft to care for her nieces and nephews. "What a treasure you have in Lucy—" Mr. Dodgson's aunt wrote to him, "that kind & excellent creature whose whole heart is now wrapped up in you & whose life will be devoted to your children." The children loved Aunt Lucy dearly, but no one could replace their mother.

A grieving Charles returned to Christ Church. Despite his loss, he was determined to make the best of his time at the university. Oxford distracted him, "that sweet city" of old

25

gray stone, famous for its "dreaming spires." The university was made up of nineteen colleges, spread throughout the town, each with its own buildings and grounds.

Wherever they went, in colleges or on city streets, college men (women were not allowed to attend British universities at this time) wore black caps and gowns. Undergraduates of noble birth had gold tassels on their hats. Others, called commoners, like Charles, wore black. Servitors, who worked their way through college, had no tassels at all.

Rules, like tassels, varied for students of different classes. Nobles and gentleman commoners, who paid twice as much as other undergraduates, lived leisurely lives, drinking hard,

In 1866 poet Matthew Arnold described Oxford as "That sweet city with her dreaming spires" for its lovely towers and steeples. This 1799 picture shows Christ Church with its Meadow and river path.

sleeping late, hunting often, and playing at sports. Reading students, like Charles, studied diligently.

Soon after returning to Christ Church, nineteen-year-old Charles moved to two rooms of his own overlooking Peckwater Quad, an interior courtyard. His day began with a breakfast of chops or sausages prepared by a servant, or "scout," and served in his rooms. Each scout took care of students on one or more staircases of a two- or three-story building.

After chapel, two hours of lectures, a light lunch, and time spent reading and studying, Charles usually took a long walk. Setting off across green meadows at the edge of town, or following a path by the river, he often covered twenty miles a day.

Christ Church undergraduates ate their dinner "in Hall," in a huge, oak-paneled dining room with high vaulted ceilings. Seating was by class: nobles sat at High Table, the others below. Meals, notoriously bad, were served on pewter plates, with a joint of meat passed around for each man to carve for himself. Dining in Hall was expensive but obligatory, as attendance was taken at dinner and at chapel rather than in class.

Evenings found Charles studying, writing letters, or recording the day's events in his diary. He began keeping a journal as an undergraduate and continued the practice for the rest of his life.

When Charles arrived at Oxford, the university, like Rugby, was modernizing its curriculum. In addition to classics and mathematics, Oxford offered French and German, history, and law. Art and music were also taught, although many scorned these as subjects for women. The inclusion of science was hotly debated, even though scientific innovations, such as the steam engine, were transforming the way people lived. Conservative faculty judged science to be too practical and insufficiently intellectual for university study.

Meanwhile, in London, a great display opened to celebrate industrial achievements based on scientific discoveries. July 5, 1851, found Charles in the nation's capital city, which was just a morning's train ride from Oxford. He had come to see the Great Exhibition, a trade fair organized by Britain, the world's leading industrial power. By showing the work and art of many nations, the fair extended business opportunities. Varying entrance fees on different days meant both rich and poor could attend. The Great Exhibition was one of the first events in England to include all social classes.

With a streaming crowd, Charles made his way to the Crystal Palace, a huge but temporary iron and glass structure that covered nineteen acres in Hyde Park and housed one hundred thousand exhibits of technology and fine arts. He was one of six million people to attend the exhibition in the five months that it was open.

Queen Victoria's husband, Prince Albert, was the event's major sponsor. The queen paid a preview visit to the exhibition before it opened. "I came back quite dead beat," she wrote in her diary, "and my head really bewildered by the myriads of beautiful and wonderful things, which now quite dazzle one's eyes."

Charles agreed: "It looks like a sort of fairyland," he wrote to his sister Elizabeth. "As far as you can look in any direction, you see nothing but pillars hung about with shawls, carpets, &c., with long avenues of statues, fountains, canopies." Each country had its own exhibit.

In the United States section, one statue of a woman, called *The Greek Slave,* by artist Hiram Powers, attracted considerable attention. *Punch,* the British humor magazine, saw the irony of this subject: in the United States, slavery was legal. "We have the Greek Captive in dead stone," wrote

The rules of the Great Exhibition prohibited exhibits made with slave labor. John Tenniel's political cartoon protested slavery in the United States. His monogram initials appear at bottom right.

THE VIRGINIAN SLAVE.

Punch. "Why not the Virginian slave in living ebony?" *Punch* published a cartoon by artist John Tenniel, depicting a sad African woman in chains, posed like the woman in the statue.

In another exhibit, an Oxford furniture dealer known as the Mad Hatter, for always wearing a top hat, displayed his "Registered Alarum Bedstead." After ringing an alarm bell, this bed deposited the sleeper onto the floor. The Great Exhibition also included the world's first important exhibit of photography, which seemed miraculous to people seeing the pictures for the first time.

Back at Oxford, in December 1852, Charles was nominated for a Studentship. The position paid £25 a year and guaranteed Charles the right to live at Christ Church for life. Students were expected to become priests in the Anglican Church. They were not allowed to marry. Most Students, including Charles's father when he had been at Oxford, held the position for just a few years. Then, like Mr. Dodgson, they gave up their Studentships to marry (priests in other positions were allowed to marry) and to pursue careers as clerics in the outside world. On hearing news of the Studentship, Mr. Dodgson wrote to his son, "your affectionate heart will derive no small addition of joy from thinking of the joy which you have occasioned to me, and to all the circle of your home."

In the spring of 1854, Charles moved to two rooms at a building called the Cloisters. That summer he joined a mathematical reading party, a group of students tutored by Professor Bartholomew Price. The reading party met, but did not work overly hard, at the seaside resort of Whitby on the east coast of England. There Charles's work was published for the first time. A story and a poem under the pseudonym B. B. appeared in the *Whitby Gazette*. Charles had used the initials before in a family magazine.

In late 1854, Charles obtained First Class Honors in the Final Mathematical School [examination]. All the Whitby party had done well, but Charles topped the list. He wrote to his sister Mary:

> Enclosed you will find a list, which I expect you to rejoice over considerably... I feel at present very like a child with a new toy, but I daresay I shall be tired of it soon and wish to be the Pope of Rome next.... I

have just given my Scout a bottle of wine to drink to
my First. We shall be made Bachelors [graduated with
a bachelor's degree] on Monday.

The next autumn, Charles returned to Christ Church as a
graduate student. Even among the other black-gowned men,
he stood out. At nearly six feet, he was tall for the time, and his
thin frame and excellent posture made him appear taller still.
His hair, worn longer than the usual style, was curly and brown,
and his eyes were described as gray or blue. This charming
twenty-three-year-old listened to others with a pleasant,
crooked grin. Perhaps because of his speech hesitation,
Charles spoke slowly and precisely, in a high-pitched voice. He
sang well, had large hands, and offered a strong grip.

For the first time he began to tutor private students in
mathematics. He wrote about teaching to his youngest siblings,
Henrietta and Edwin, aged about twelve and nine.

My one pupil has begun his work with me, and I will
give you a description how the lecture is conducted. It
is the most important point, you know, that the tutor
should be *dignified,* and at a distance from the pupil,
and that the pupil should be as much as possible *de-
graded*—otherwise, you know, they are not humble
enough. So I sit at the further end of the room; outside
the door *(which is shut)* sits the scout; outside the
outer door *(also shut)* sits the sub-scout; half-way
down stairs sits the sub-sub-scout; and down in the
yard sits the *pupil.*

The questions are shouted from one to the other,
and the answers come back in the same way—it is
rather confusing till you are well used to it. The lec-
ture goes on, something like this.
Tutor. "What is twice three?"
Scout. "What's a rice tree?"
Sub-Scout. "When is ice free?"
Sub-sub-Scout. "What's a nice fee?"

Pupil (timidly). "Half a guinea!"
Sub-sub-Scout. "Can't forge any!"
Sub-Scout. "Ho for Jinny!"
Scout. "Don't be a ninny!"

Soon Charles averaged six hours a day tutoring fourteen men in algebra, Euclid (geometry), trigonometry, differential calculus, and arithmetic. "Pretty well," he commented, "for one who is *not* College Lecturer."

That same term Charles was made sub-librarian and given a small office in the Christ Church Library. It was a perfect job for Charles, who read widely—everything from popular fiction and poetry to scholarly works on serious subjects. For this part-time work he kept track of library books and their borrowers.

Feeling quite the young man about town, Charles decided to begin the long holiday of 1855 with a trip to London. There he attended the annual Royal Academy exhibition, where the most prominent British artists displayed their works.

Similarly he began a tradition of theatergoing. Of a performance of Shakespeare's *Henry VIII* at the Princess Theatre, he wrote:

> Oh, that exquisite vision of Queen Catherine! I almost held my breath to watch: the illusion is perfect, and I felt as if in a dream all the time it lasted. . . . This is the true end and object of acting—to raise the mind above itself, and out of its petty everyday cares.

At home that summer, Charles compiled a scrapbook, called *Mischmasch,* of his best work, published or unpublished. It included what he called "an obscure, but yet deeply-affecting [sic.], relic of ancient Poetry":

TWAS BRYLLYG, AND THE SLYTHY TOVES
DID GYRE AND GYMBLE IN THE WABE:
ALL MIMSY WERE THE BOROGOVES;
AND THE MOME RATHS OUTGRABE.

The words were Charles's tongue-in-cheek imitation of Anglo-Saxon, or Old English. Helpfully he provided a translation: "It was evening, and the smooth active badgers were scratching and boring holes in the hill-side: all unhappy were the parrots; and the grave turtles squeaked out."

Charles was thrilled when his uncle, Skeffington Lutwidge, came to Croft with a wonderful new gadget: a camera. When Charles was born, in 1832, only an artist could capture a likeness. Portraits were expensive and rare. Newspapers and books contained drawings by artists that had been turned into engravings, but these, too, were costly and not readily available.

In the 1700s and early 1800s, scientists had captured fleeting images on light- sensitive paper but found no way to make them last. In 1839, when Charles was seven, a British scientist had found a way to "fix" images permanently. William Henry Fox Talbot invented negatives that could be used to print many copies of the same picture.

Early photographic methods were protected by patents, but in the 1850s a newly discovered technique, the wet collodion method, became available for public use. Charles studied his uncle's equipment: the heavy camera, glass plates, tripod, and suitcases full of chemicals. The would-be artist was thrilled to discover a new and reliable way of creating images.

In August 1855, Charles was appointed Mathematical Lecturer (the principal tutor of mathematics) at Christ Church. On October 15, he was made a Master of the House, though he did not actually receive his master's degree until 1857.

In 1863 Charles photographed his sisters with croquet mallets in the Croft Rectory garden. People look serious in early photographs because long exposure times (up to one minute) made it difficult to hold a smile.

As his academic career progressed, Charles began writing humorous pieces for a London magazine called *The Train.* Perhaps to protect his academic reputation, he published these under his earlier pseudonym, B. B. Editor Edmund Yates asked for a better name.

Yates rejected Dares for Daresbury, so Charles suggested four other possibilities. Edgar Cuthwellis or Edgar U. C. Westhill were anagrams, formed from the letters of his forenames, Charles Lutwidge. Louis Carroll and Lewis Carroll were Latinized versions of these same names, reversed and re-anglicized—Louis and Lewis from Ludovicus

(Latin for Lutwidge) and Carroll from Carolus (Latin for Charles). It was Yates who picked the name Lewis Carroll. On New Year's Eve, 1855, Charles wrote in his diary:

> I am sitting alone in my bedroom this last night of the old year, waiting for midnight. It has been the most eventful year of my life: I began it a poor bachelor student, with no definite plans or expectations; I end it a master and tutor in Ch. Ch., with an income of more than £300 a year, and the course of mathematical tuition marked out by God's providence for at least some years to come.

With children, Charles spoke easily, but in other situations, his speech impediment caused problems. He read aloud a scene from Shakespeare every day, in a lifelong effort to improve his speech.

Chapter Four

White Stone Days
1856–1860

Charles began the 1856 winter term with a problem: his students. Although undergraduates were required to take mathematics, some did not seem interested. "Of the 60 men sent for," he wrote in his diary, "only 23 appeared." He was also teaching two classes of "sums" (arithmetic) at a local school. "School class again noisy and troublesome," he reported. "I have not yet acquired the art of keeping order."

In happier moments, Charles, and all of Oxford, anticipated the arrival of the new dean of Christ Church. Henry George Liddell (rhymes with "fiddle"), a respected clergyman and educator, was famous as coauthor of a Greek lexicon. Charles knew the lexicon well, having ordered it for himself while in school. From his office at the Christ Church Library, Charles had a good view of the Deanery garden. He could watch workmen going in and out as they readied the house for its new occupants.

On February 25, at a boat race, Charles met Mrs. Lorina Liddell and her two eldest children, Harry and Lorina, aged eight and six. Mrs. Liddell was a beauty with dark hair and eyes—a lively, jolly woman who enjoyed bringing people together. Soon, the Liddells gave their first party, divided over two evenings to accommodate the many guests. Charles, invited for the second night, chatted happily with young Lorina, and soon Harry and Lorina began visiting Mr. Dodgson in his rooms.

Easter vacation found Charles in London, where he ordered a camera. That same evening he heard the famous soprano Jenny Lind sing. In his journal Charles wrote, "This day I mark with a white stone," a phrase he used to note a memorable day.

Back in Oxford, Charles helped his friend, Reginald Southey, who was already an accomplished photographer. Charles wrote:

> Went over with Southey in the afternoon to the Deanery, to try and take a photograph of the Cathedral: both attempts proved failures. The three little girls were in the garden most of the time, and we became excellent friends: we tried to group them in the foreground of the picture but they were not patient sitters. I mark this day with a white stone.

The three little girls were Lorina and her younger sisters, Alice, aged almost four, and Edith, about two.

Charles's own camera and chemicals, which cost him a month's salary, arrived at Christ Church on May 1. Soon he had mastered the complex method of taking pictures—mixing chemicals, pouring them carefully onto glass plates, exposing the plates to light, and finally bathing them in chemical solutions to make negatives.

For Charles, and all Victorians, the impact of photography was staggering. It opened new worlds, as television and the Internet would do in the next century. To Charles its most exciting potential was artistic. The principles he had studied all his life as he sketched—design, perspective, contrast—applied equally well to this new, scientific art form, and no drawing talent was required!

Throughout the summer, Charles photographed the Liddell children. Sometimes he invited Harry and Lorina on outings. After a lively boat trip, he wrote, "fortunately, considering the wild spirits of the children, we got home without accident."

Charles took this 1858 photograph in the Deanery garden, using a blanket as a backdrop. Left to right: *Edith, Lorina, and Alice, aged about four, nine, and six.*

In autumn 1856, Charles's brothers Skeffington and Wilfred, aged about twenty and eighteen, began study at Christ Church. Soon Charles was including his brothers in excursions with the Liddells. Charles knew the whole family now, even the cat, Dinah, who sometimes had to be chased from the library.

He was glad to have interests beyond teaching. "I am weary of lecturing and discouraged," he wrote. "It is thankless uphill work, goading unwilling men to learning they have no taste for, to the inevitable neglect of others who really want to get on." Better textbooks would help, Charles decided, and he began work on a series of books to make mathematics more interesting.

In a letter to a childfriend, Charles wrote, "What I look like when I'm lecturing," to describe the selfportrait he included with the letter.

In winter, when the light grew too faint for photography, Charles still thought about taking pictures. Now he studied paintings in a new way. "I took hasty sketches," he wrote, after attending a London art exhibit, "chiefly for the arrangement of hands, to help in grouping for photographs." For group poses, Charles noted, one must give "to the different figures one object of attention."

The Liddell children were often left in the care of their governess, who welcomed Charles's help in amusing them. On May 17, 1857, Charles reported:

> Took Harry Liddell to chapel, and afterwards walked back with the children to the Deanery. I find to my great surprise that my notice of them is construed by some men into attentions to the governess, Miss Prickett . . . and though for my own part I should give little importance to the existence of so groundless a rumour, it would be inconsiderate to the governess to give any further occasion for remarks of the sort.

Still, he visited the Deanery. "Harry was away," he wrote three weeks later, "but the two dear little girls, Ina [a nickname for Lorina] and Alice, were with me all the morning. To try the lens, I took a picture of myself, for which Ina took off the cap, and of course considered it all her doing!"

That summer the Liddells let Charles leave his photographic equipment set up in the Deanery garden. Often he had furniture and blankets carried out, using them as backdrops so that his pictures seemed to have been taken indoors. To relax his young models, he told them stories, as he had told them to his sisters and brothers.

"When we were thoroughly happy and amused," Alice recalled later, "he used to pose us, and expose the plates before the right mood had passed." Of the three sisters, she was the best model, as Lorina did not particularly like being photographed and Edith could not hold still. Charles's most famous photograph of Alice, taken when she was six, shows her dressed as a beggar maid. They were pretending, she explained later, that she was the Little Match Girl from the Hans Christian Andersen story.

Though the beautiful Liddell children were his favorite subjects, Charles also photographed family and friends. Using

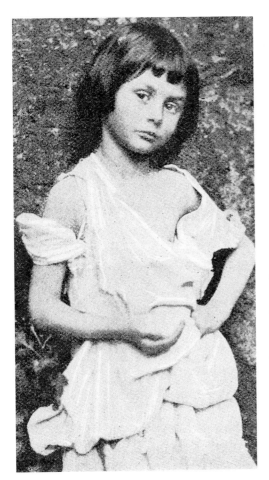

Alice as a beggar, Charles's most famous photograph, taken in 1858 when she was six. Some modern interpretations judged this pose and costume to be seductive and, therefore, controversial.

simple backgrounds, he focused attention on his models. In group shots, he made sure that each head was on a different level. Portraiture and composition became his special talents.

The popularity of photography created a prosperous industry in England. Within a few years, "glass houses," or photographers' studios, dotted the London skyline. These structures made indoor pictures possible, even in winter, by letting in light and keeping out the cold.

Throughout Britain, shops opened to sell photographs and equipment. The *carte de visite,* or small, business-card-sized portrait, was introduced in 1857, at prices almost anyone could afford. Cartes of the royal family proved so popular that stores offered pictures of celebrities. Soon famous people were hounded to sit for photographers.

Shopkeepers began selling special albums for cartes. The finest such books were bound in leather, and some even played music when opened. Every Victorian drawing room, including Charles's sitting room at Christ Church, had an album for visitors to enjoy. The first pages usually featured the royal family, then people admired by the owner, and, finally, relatives and friends. "I have got the whole set of the Royal Family," Charles wrote to Croft, "and will bring them home with me."

He began to think that photography might give him a chance to meet famous people. In August 1857, a Mrs. Weld brought her young daughter Agnes to the Croft Rectory to be photographed. Mrs. Weld's sister was the wife of Alfred, Lord Tennyson, Poet Laureate of England and one of Charles's favorite authors.

Photographing Agnes as Little Red Riding-Hood, Charles gave Mrs. Weld an extra copy of the picture for her famous in-law. Soon Mrs. Weld wrote that Tennyson had pronounced the portrait "indeed a gem."

Later that summer, Charles went hiking in the Lake District, a popular vacation spot in the northwest of England. He learned that Tennyson was staying nearby, at a place called Tent Lodge. "I . . . made up my mind to take the liberty of calling," Charles wrote. "I sent in my card, adding underneath the name in pencil, 'Artist of Agnes Grace' and 'Little Red Riding-hood.'"

Soon Charles met the famous poet, whom he described as "a strange shaggy-looking man." Charles was thrilled to be able to ask the author about his famous poem "Maud."

Invited for dinner at Tent Lodge, Charles brought an album of his own photographs to show. "I left at what I believed to be a little after 9," he wrote, "but which to my horror I found to be at least 11, having had a most interesting and delightful evening. The hotel was shut up for the night, and I had to wait and ring a long time while at the door."

Two years later, again uninvited, Charles called on Tennyson at his home on the Isle of Wight, an island resort off the south coast of England. On this visit, the poet told Charles that he sometimes dreamed long passages of poetry. "You, I suppose," Tennyson said, turning to Charles, "dream photographs."

Charles photographed the Tennyson family, and they introduced him to their neighbor, Julia Margaret Cameron. An amateur photographer like Charles, Mrs. Cameron was becoming known for her portraits. Short and stout, dressed in red and purple draperies, wearing robes spotted with photographic chemical stains, she made her home, Dimbola Lodge, a gathering place for artists and writers. Charles's relationship with Tennyson never developed into real friendship, but the two photographers maintained a cordial acquaintance for many years.

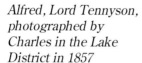

Alfred, Lord Tennyson,
photographed by
Charles in the Lake
District in 1857

In 1860 Charles consulted a doctor for help with his speech hesitation. Through him Charles met the Scottish author George MacDonald, a stammerer, who had just published his first story for children.

Later, at the London studio of his friend Alexander Munro, a sculptor, Charles met, for the first time, two of MacDonald's children. Watched by his sister Mary, young Greville MacDonald was posing for the artist. Munro's sculpture of Greville, *Boy with a Dolphin,* can still be seen in London's Hyde Park. Charles recalled the meeting:

They were a girl and a boy, about seven and six years old—I claimed their acquaintance and began at once proving to the boy, Greville, that he had better take the opportunity of having his head changed for a marble one. The effect was that in about two minutes they had entirely forgotten that I was a total stranger, and were earnestly arguing the question as if we were old acquaintances.

About this same time, Charles met some important scientists when they came to Oxford to debate the work of Charles Darwin. In the previous year, 1859, Darwin's book

Charles probably used a timing device to take this picture of himself with the MacDonalds. Left to right: Louisa (Mrs. MacDonald), Greville, Mary, Charles, Irene, Grace.

On the Origin of Species by Means of Natural Selection had caused a sensation. Darwin had studied generations of plants and animals. Like farmers, he knew that cattle could be bred to increase milk production. Darwin called this process "controlled" selection. In natural selection, he theorized, individuals who were best suited to their environments survived, while others less fit got weeded out. Natural selection, Darwin believed, created new species that could not breed with each other.

His beliefs clashed with those of leading scholars. Many of them were clergymen who believed that God had created each individual species, and that no species could change or evolve. To them, Darwin's ideas threatened religion and denied the existence of God. Darwinism, claimed critics, taught that man was descended from apes.

More than seven hundred men, but not Darwin himself, attended the "apes and angels" debate. It seems likely that Charles went too. He certainly served on the reception committee for visiting scientists, using the occasion to photograph some of them. When Darwin's supporters won the debate, their victory helped change the thinking of scientists around the world.

On December 12, 1860, the ultimate celebrity, Queen Victoria, visited Christ Church. "I . . . was shocked," wrote Charles, "to find how short, not to say dumpy, and (with all loyalty be it spoken), how *plain* she is. She is *exactly* like the little full-length photograph published of her."

"*The Rabbit started violently, dropped the white kid gloves and the fan, and skurried away into the darkness as hard as he could go.*"
(*Illustration by* John Tenniel *for* Alice's Adventures in Wonderland)

Chapter Five

Alice's Adventures under Ground

1860–1864

On New Year's Eve, 1857, Charles had written:

> Five minutes more, and the Old Year comes to an end, leaving how many of its promises unfulfilled! . . . What do I propose as the work of the New Year? . . . Reading for Ordination at the end of the year, and settling the subject finally and definitely in my mind.

Settling the subject proved difficult: three years later, at age twenty-nine, Charles still felt ambivalent about becoming a priest. Ordination, though required of Students at Christ Church, seemed irrelevant to the duties of a mathematical tutor.

To Charles, the priest's duty of representing the Church, mediating between people and God, was a matter of profound importance. Despite his strong faith, he worried that he was not suited for the work. How could a man with a speech hesitation preach a sermon or read from the Bible? His handicap, Charles believed, would distract from God's message.

On reflection, Charles realized that he no longer believed every part of the Church's Thirty-Nine Articles of Faith, which he had signed when matriculating at Christ Church. How could he honestly represent the Anglican Church's unchanging viewpoint?

The Church's position on the theater, although not addressed in the Articles, worried Charles greatly. Many prominent clergymen, including his father, thought the theater was immoral. Charles believed that the theater, like books, could be used for good or evil. He chose plays carefully, and if something on the stage offended him, he walked out. Following his own rules, for many years Charles had attended most major performances in London. How could he become a minister when he adored the theater?

After much worry, Charles chose to take holy orders. He was ordained a deacon on December 22, 1861. The Reverend Mr. Dodgson, as Charles was known after this ceremony, held the lowest rank of clergy in the Anglican Church. As a deacon, Charles had no particular duties. The requirements for Students to become priests dated from medieval times when Oxford had been strictly a religious institution.

But Charles took the responsibility of his new title seriously, volunteering to help his father and his priest friends, preaching sermons in their churches, or leading services when they were called away. He dressed as a clergyman in a black frock coat with a loosely tied white cravat. He wore his top hat set well back on his head. Once ordained, Charles was granted another year in which to decide about becoming a priest.

Confident now as a teacher, he had published a book, *A Syllabus of Plane Algebraical Geometry,* the first of many mathematical texts he would write. In early 1862, he moved to new quarters in the northwest corner of Tom Quad, the main courtyard of Christ Church. Across the green lawn was the front door of the Deanery.

Charles's happiest hours were spent with the Liddells, who had a new baby sister named Rhoda. Harry was often away at school, but Charles played croquet and cards with the three older girls, and he continued to photograph them. Sometimes, with a friend or a brother, he took them boating on the river.

Throughout his life, Charles remained thin and fit. He ate sparingly, having just a glass of wine and a biscuit for lunch. For dinner he liked mutton chops and meringues, followed by tea.

Many a day we rowed together on that quiet stream [Charles recalled later] and many a fairy tale had been extemporised . . . yet none of these many tales got written down . . . until there came a day, when . . . one of my little listeners petitioned that the tale might be written out for her. . . . I . . . remember . . . how, in a desperate attempt to strike out some new line of fairy-lore, I had sent my heroine straight down a rabbit-hole, to begin with, without the least idea what was to happen afterwards.

Leaving Oxford for the long vacation, Charles traveled and took pictures. He photographed another Alice, eleven-year-old Alice Jane Donkin, niece of an Oxford professor. Charles's memorable picture, which he titled "The Elopement," showed his subject as a bride-to-be, escaping from her bedroom window with a rope ladder.

"The Elopement." Charles called this photograph of Alice Donkin a "composition-picture." Like other Victorian photographers, he dressed his subjects in costumes and posed them to illustrate stories.

Meanwhile Charles anguished over becoming a less-than-perfect priest, revealing in his diary self-doubt and strong feelings of unworthiness. Finally, he called on Dean Liddell, to ask if he was obliged to take priest's orders. Yes, said the Dean, but then, surprisingly, he changed his mind, deciding to make an exception to the rules. The decision allowed Charles to remain a deacon for life, with a secure job and a home at Christ Church.

Throughout the winter, Charles worked on his story for Alice Liddell. Curious to know whether the tale would amuse children, he consulted his friend George MacDonald. MacDonald's son Greville, who had posed for the *Boy with a Dolphin* sculpture, recalled later that: "My mother read the story to us. When she came to an end I, being aged six, exclaimed that there ought to be sixty thousand volumes of it."

About this time, Charles met the publisher Alexander Macmillan. Macmillan, who had recently published the best-selling fairy tale, *The Water-Babies,* was interested in Charles's book.

In March 1863, Charles and all of England celebrated the marriage of Queen Victoria's oldest son, Albert, Prince of Wales, to Princess Alexandra of Denmark. Charles's youngest brother, Edwin, now about seventeen, came to Christ Church from Croft for the festivities.

On the wedding day, Charles wrote, "Called at the Deanery at 10, to arrange about our expedition tonight, and to borrow a Natural History to help in illustrating 'Alice's Adventures.'" He needed the book as a guide for drawing the many animals he had included in his story.

Later Alice recalled that evening: "Mr. Dodgson and his brother took me out to see the illuminations [fireworks]. The crowd in the streets was very great, and I clung tightly on to the hand of the strong man on either side of me."

"The Wedding-day of the Prince of Wales," wrote Charles in his diary, "I mark with a white stone."

In June the prince brought his bride to the Deanery for a three-day visit, part of their honeymoon tour. The house bustled with preparations, and Charles was allowed to look at the bedroom that had been readied for them. Noticing a magnificent carte de visite album, he offered to fill it with pictures and spent several hours arranging his own photographs.

At Christ Church, the prince and princess played croquet with the young Liddells. The children also sat with the royal couple on a platform erected for an outdoor ceremony in Tom Quad. Charles watched the program from the rooms of his lifelong friend Thomas Vere Bayne. Bayne broke out the pane of a window so that Charles could set up his telescope for a better view of the royal guests.

On June 25, 1863, Charles arranged a river excursion for the Liddells—the Dean, Mrs. Liddell, Lorina, Alice, Edith, and little Rhoda—with two other men and Charles himself. Though he did not realize it, this happy day marked the end of their boating trips.

His diary entry for June 27, 1863, ends with an unfinished sentence: "Wrote to Mrs. Liddell urging her . . . to send the children to be photographed."

The following page from Charles's diary is missing, most likely cut out by a relative after his death, to avoid embarrassment for Charles or the family. Probably Charles had recorded a request from Dean and Mrs. Liddell that he spend less time with the girls. This lost page and other missing portions of Charles's diary have led to more than one hundred years of speculation. A paper in the family archives appears to be an extract of the missing page: "L.C. learns from Mrs. Liddell that he is supposed to be using the children as a means of paying court to the governess. He is also supposed by some to be courting Ina."

Charles's friend Lord Salisbury insisted later that eleven-year-old Alice, not fourteen-year-old Lorina, was the focus of Charles's interest. Many years after, Lorina wrote to Alice about Charles: "his manner became too affectionate to you as you grew older and . . . mother spoke to him about it, and that offended him so he ceased coming to visit us again."

Some biographers have speculated that Charles was in love with Alice. In a situation like this, a man might give notice to the girl's parents of his intent to court her later. The age gap (he was twenty years older than Alice) was acceptable. Like Mrs. Liddell, who was fifteen years younger than the Dean, young women of social standing often married older men who were established in their careers. But the Liddells expected their daughters to marry men of wealth and status. In these respects, Charles did not qualify.

Though Charles saw less of the Liddells after this time, he continued to work on his story for Alice. His social life became centered in London, in a witty circle of writers and artists. George MacDonald, his wife, and eleven children welcomed "Uncle Dodgson" like a beloved relative. Charles loved all the children, but Mary became a favorite correspondent and the recipient of some of his most charming letters:

> My dear Child,
> It's been so frightfully hot here that I've been almost too weak to hold a pen, and even if I had been able, there was no ink—it had all evaporated into a cloud of black steam, and in that state it has been floating about the room, inking the walls and ceiling till they're hardly fit to be seen.

Sculptor Alexander Munro let Charles set up photo-graphic equipment at his London home. Through Munro, Charles met a new friend, Tom Taylor, a playwright and con-tributor to *Punch,* the humor magazine. Alexander Munro also took Charles to Tudor House, the home of Dante Gabriel Rosetti, the artist and poet. Rosetti's pets included an owl, a woodchuck, a deer, and a wombat that sometimes fell asleep on the dinner table.

"With such inhabitants," wrote the poet's sister Christina, "Tudor House and its grounds became a sort of wonderland; and once the author of *Wonderland* photographed us in the garden." Christina Rosetti, also a poet, had recently published a children's book, *Goblin Market,* a long poem about children kidnapped by goblins.

In December 1863, Charles attended Christ Church Theatricals. "Mrs. Liddell and the children were there," he wrote, "but I held aloof from them as I have done all this term." Two weeks later, he relented, spending an evening at the Deanery with Mrs. Liddell and the children (the Dean was not at home) and marking the day in his diary with a white stone.

At Croft on New Year's Eve 1863, Charles wrote in his diary:

> Here, at the close of another year, how much of ne-glect carelessness, and sin have I to remember! I had hoped, during this year, to have made a beginning in parochial work [parish work, as a priest], to have thrown off habits of evil, to have advanced in my work at Ch. Ch.—how little, next to nothing, has been done of all this! Now I have a fresh year before me: once more let me set myself to do some thing worthy of life "before I go hence, and be no more seen."

His fresh start in the new year proved upsetting to Dean

Liddell. In early 1864, Liddell issued a notice about Studentship awards in mathematics, and Charles complained about the Dean's wording. A "disagreeable correspondence" followed, with Liddell calling Charles's objections "hyper-critical and unnecessary."

Two months later, as a baby girl, Violet, was born at the Deanery, Charles again angered Dean Liddell by publicly criticizing a new university statute. This policy allowed science undergraduates to omit studies of classics and created the new Third Class Degree. Charles complained that lower standards diminished the value of all Oxford degrees.

Charles discussed these issues, and many others of the day, in the Common Room, a gathering place for lecturers. Here Charles and his clever colleagues wrote "squibs," parodies that poked fun at current events. "Squib" was the name for a small firecracker. The slang term seemed appropriate for publications that sparked explosions of gossip in Oxford.

On November 26, 1864, Charles presented his handwritten manuscript to twelve-year-old Alice as an early Christmas present. *Alice's Adventures under Ground,* illustrated with Charles's drawings, was ninety-one pages long. The book begins:

> Alice was beginning to get very tired of sitting by her sister on the bank and of having nothing to do: once or twice she had peeped into the book her sister was reading, but it had no pictures or conversations in it, and where is the use of a book, thought Alice, without pictures or conversations?

When a white rabbit runs by, looking at its pocket watch, Alice follows it down a rabbit hole, falling into an underground land. There she tries to enter a locked, walled garden, like the many beautiful gardens in Oxford.

In this magic land, as Alice drinks and eats, her size changes dramatically. Grown to more than nine feet high, she cries a great pool of tears. Shrinking to three inches, she nearly drowns in the water. Soon animals fall into the pool with her—a Mouse, Duck, Dodo, Lory (a kind of parrot), Eaglet, and other creatures. With Alice leading the way, the party swims to shore, and later the Mouse tells the others a tale. Charles wrote and spaced this story on the page so that the words made a picture of a real tail.

In his story for Alice, Charles invented an unusual game: "the croquet-balls were live hedgehogs, the mallets live ostriches." (Illustration by Charles for Alice's Adventures under Ground*)*

As the story continues, Alice gets stuck in the rabbit's house. She encounters a giant puppy and meets a large blue caterpillar that is smoking a hookah, or water pipe.

Inside the beautiful garden at last, Alice discovers live playing cards. She plays croquet with the King and Queen of Hearts, meets a Gryphon and a Mock Turtle, and attends the trial of the Knave of Hearts. When the whole pack of cards comes flying down on her, Alice awakens to find herself back on the riverbank with her sister, under leaves fluttering down from the trees onto her face.

Throughout the story, Alice maintains her poise and manners, even when confronted by trying circumstances. "Curiouser and curiouser!" she cries as she grows suddenly larger, "so surprised that she quite forgot how to speak good English."

Dreamlike, she tries to remember her lessons, but the words come out wrong. Poems get mixed up, too: "How doth the little busy bee/Improve each shining hour," becomes "How doth the little crocodile/Improve its shining tail," when Alice tries to recite it. The popular song, "Star of the Evening," which the Liddell sisters sang, becomes "Soup of the evening, beautiful Soup," when sung by the Mock Turtle.

Alice and her sisters loved this book, which they read over and over. They kept it on a table in the Deanery sitting room to show to guests. Encouraged by his friends, Charles set about getting it published.

For the published version of his story, Charles changed the croquet mallets from ostriches to flamingoes. (Illustration by John Tenniel for Alice's Adventures in Wonderland*)*

Chapter Six

Alice's Adventures in Wonderland

1864–1870

Do you know Mr. Tenniel well enough," Charles asked his friend, the writer Tom Taylor, about the artist John Tenniel:

> to be able to say whether he could undertake such a thing as drawing a dozen wood-cuts to illustrate a child's book, and if so, could you put me into communication with him? The reasons for which I ask . . . are that I have written such a tale for a young friend, and illustrated it in pen and ink. . . . I have tried my hand at drawing on the wood . . . and come to the conclusion . . . that the result would not be satisfactory after all.

Taylor, who wrote for *Punch,* did know John Tenniel, the magazine's primary cartoonist.

With a note from Taylor, Charles called on Tenniel at his London home. He found a large man, aged forty-four, courteous and reserved. "He was very friendly," wrote Charles, "and seemed to think favourably of undertaking the pictures, but must see the book before deciding."

Tenniel had proved his ability to draw animals with a successful version of *Aesop's Fables*. He was best known for his creation of the British Lion, used as Britain's national symbol, like Uncle Sam in the United States.

Three months later, Tenniel accepted Charles's proposal, and Charles agreed to Tenniel's asking fee of £148. Charles had also struck a deal with publisher Alexander Macmillan: Charles would employ the illustrator, the engravers (to carve the wood blocks used in printing the illustrations), and the printer. The publisher, Macmillan, would distribute the book for 10 percent of the receipts.

Charles began rewriting his text, removing jokes that were understandable only to his friends, and eventually doubling the length. He designed the book himself, telling Tenniel what to draw, often requesting improved versions of his own illustrations.

Worried that Tenniel, who was a childless widower, had little experience drawing children, Charles tried to get the artist to work from a model. Tenniel, said Charles, "declared he no more needed one than I should need a multiplication-table to work a mathematical problem!"

Author and artist argued amiably over how their heroine should look and whether she should have a fringe (bangs). Both men drew Alice with long, wavy hair, looking more like popular artists' models of the day than the real Alice. Both were meticulous, requesting of each other and the engravers many small changes, which delayed publication.

As the work progressed, Charles entered into a public dispute with Dean Liddell. Charles and his fellow Christ Church Students demanded, and later won, a say in how the

Contrary to some published reports, John Tenniel, right, and Charles got along well. Their friendly, professional relationship lasted to the end of Charles's life.

college was run. Charles's squib, *American Telegrams,* reported the struggle as news dispatches from the Civil War that was being waged in the United States. This spoof featured President L (Dean Liddell) and the Confederate Commissioners (disgruntled Students).

At the same time, Charles was considering titles for his book: should he call it "Alice Among the Goblins," "Alice's Hour in Elf-land," or "Alice's Adventures in Wonderland"? He arranged for Oxford University Press to print the pages, which Macmillan would bind. Choosing red for the cover, as most attractive to children, Charles asked Macmillan for one special copy to be bound in white vellum, or fine leather, for Alice Liddell.

With the book in production, Charles made his rounds in London. "Went to the Photographic Exhibition," he wrote. "I did *not* admire Mrs. Cameron's large heads taken out of focus." Like Charles, Julia Margaret Cameron photographed many celebrities, including Ellen Terry, a beautiful young actress who was one of Charles's favorites.

Charles had recognized Ellen Terry's talent the first time he saw her, in 1856, when she was just nine years old. At that time, she was appearing in Shakespeare's *A Winter's Tale* with her sister Kate, aged twelve. Charles had followed the girls' careers as Kate grew into starring roles, and Ellen seemed poised to follow.

Then, at the age of sixteen, Ellen had retired from the stage to marry a forty-six-year-old artist, G. F. Watts. His rich and powerful friends disapproved of the match. After ten months, shockingly, Watts sent his young wife back to her parents. In the summer of 1865, the beautiful seventeen-year-old was working with playwright Tom Taylor, planning a return to the stage.

With another letter of introduction from Taylor, Charles called at the Terrys' London home, and at a later time he met Kate and Ellen. "I was very much pleased with what I saw of Mrs. Watts," he wrote, "lively and pleasant, almost childish in her face, but perfectly ladylike. . . . I mark this day also with a white stone."

Charles may have felt relieved to find the actress ladylike, since her separation from her husband was considered disgraceful. Charles began visiting the Terrys regularly, playing croquet with Ellen, Kate, and their younger sisters. The Terrys gave him tickets for plays, to which he invited the younger Terry girls and also the MacDonald children.

On July 15, 1865, Charles called at Macmillan's London

office. For the first time, he held a printed, bound copy of *Alice's Adventures in Wonderland*. Charles inscribed more than twenty books, asking Macmillan to mail them to certain of his friends.

Tenniel, however, was not happy with the work. "He is entirely dissatisfied with the printing of the pictures," wrote Charles, "and I suppose we shall have to do it all again."

The Oxford University Press had printed the book too hastily. On some pages, where words and pictures were printed back to back, words showed through the illustrations. Other pictures were faint, lacking detail. Tenniel worried that the sloppy printing might damage his reputation.

Agreeing with his illustrator, Charles paid to have all two thousand copies of the book reprinted, but some of the presentation copies had already been mailed. Of this first printing, twenty-three books, including Alice's, are known to have survived, now some of the rarest and most sought after books in publishing history.

Later, at Tenniel's suggestion, Charles had the rejected books bound with a new title page and sold as the first American edition. Apparently the artist did not worry about his reputation in America.

As Charles waited for the book to be reissued, he worked as a deacon. In 1865 he preached twenty sermons, all different and all carefully prepared. In Croft he counseled his own family when his brother Wilfred, aged twenty-seven, revealed that he had fallen in love with Alice Jane Donkin, aged fourteen. Charles had photographed her years before, as an eloping bride. Now, convinced that she was too young for marriage, and knowing that Wilfred lacked the income to support a wife, Charles hoped that she would not really elope! He was relieved when Wilfred followed his advice to wait.

In December 1865, the new edition of *Alice,* dated 1866, was published. The pictures were "very *far* superior to the old," according to Charles.

Charles used the same framework for this book as for Alice's original manuscript but added new scenes and characters: a cook who uses too much pepper and an ugly Duchess, nursing a baby. When Alice holds the baby, it changes to a pig. A grinning Cheshire Cat, resembling the real Alice's Dinah, fades in and out of view, perched on a tree limb, just as Dinah sat in the chestnut tree in the Deanery garden.

"This time it vanished quite slowly, beginning with the end of the tail, and ending with the grin, which remained some time after the rest of it had gone." (The Cheshire Cat, by John Tenniel for Alice's Adventures in Wonderland)

As in the handwritten, original version, Alice maintains her composure. She asserts her opinions politely, even at a mad tea party with a Hatter, a March Hare, and a Dormouse who falls asleep at the table, like Dante Gabriel Rosetti's pet wombat.

New parodies of songs and rhymes appear, like "Twinkle, Twinkle, Little Bat." Puns abound, as in the Mock Turtle's account of his school at the bottom of the sea. His studies, he tells Alice, include "Reeling and Writhing . . . and then the different branches of Arithmetic—Ambition, Distraction, Uglification, and Derision."

Tenniel's woodcuts provided the perfect balance of formality and silliness. They complemented Charles's text, adding immensely to the book's appeal.

First reactions arrived quickly from friends. Christina Rosetti wrote to Charles:

> A thousand and one thanks . . . for the funny pretty book you have so very kindly sent me. My Mother and Sister as well as myself made ourselves quite at home yesterday in Wonderland . . . I confess it would give me sincere pleasure to fall in with that conversational rabbit. . . . The woodcuts are charming.

Her famous brother wrote of Charles's book, "The wonderful ballad of Father William and Alice's perverted snatches of school poetry are among the funniest things I have seen for a long while."

But it was published book reviews, Charles knew, that would predict the sales to come. Soon he had reason to celebrate. The *Sunderland Herald* said, "This very pretty and funny book . . . has this advantage, that it has no moral, and that it does not teach anything. It is, in fact, pure sugar throughout." The *Publisher's Circular* named it "the most original and most charming" children's book of the year.

In June 1866, the happy author invited his family for a fortnight's holiday at the seaside resort of Whitby. Charles wrote to Aunt Lucy:

> How many go, and which, is a question I leave entirely to the sisterhood to settle among themselves: with them I include you (who I hope will be able to come) and Edwin. I need not offer to treat Skeffington, being now a gentleman of independent income.

Skeffington had become the curate, or assistant clergyman, to their father at Croft.

Alice's Adventures in Wonderland sold so well that within one year, Charles began to earn profits. "I have ... a floating idea," he wrote to Macmillan, "of writing a sort of sequel." But when he approached his illustrator about a second volume, Tenniel declined, pleading overwork. Calling on several other artists, Charles found none to please him. Joseph Noel Paton, who had illustrated *The Water-Babies,* refused the project on grounds of ill health. "Tenniel is *the* man," Paton advised Charles.

With the situation unresolved, Charles made unusual summer plans for 1867, setting off for Russia with a friend from undergraduate days. The Reverend Henry Parry Liddon went partly on business, with the hope of bringing the Anglican and Russian churches closer together. Charles wanted to see the sights, especially foreign religion and art.

Crossing the English Channel by ferry, they traveled across Europe on trains. In his journal, Charles described two guiding principles of architecture he had observed in Berlin, Germany:

On the house-tops, wherever there is a convenient place, put up the figure of a man; he is best placed standing on one leg. Wherever there is room on the ground, put... the colossal figure of a man killing, about to kill, or having killed (the present tense is preferred) a beast; the more prickles the beast has, the better—in fact a dragon is the correct thing, but if that is beyond the artist, he may content himself with a lion or a pig.

From the Russian city of Nizhniy Novgorod, Charles wrote to his sister Louisa: "The great annual fair is going on... and the whole place swarms with Greeks, Jews,

Nizhniy Novgorod, Russia, where hardly anyone spoke English. Charles used a pocket dictionary to read Russian words. When words and gestures failed, he drew pictures in order to communicate.

Armenians, Persians, Chinamen, etc., besides the native Russians." He loved the "unheard-of costumes" he saw there and the call to prayer he heard from the roof of the Tartar Mosque. "Indescribably sad," he called it.

Home again, Charles celebrated new publications: a book on mathematics, *An Elementary Treatise on Determinants,* a poem in *Punch,* and "Bruno's Revenge," a fairy story in *Aunt Judy's Magazine* (for children). He learned also that his friend Robinson Duckworth had joined the royal household as tutor to Queen Victoria's youngest son. Prince Leopold, aged thirteen, was a hemophiliac, someone whose blood is very slow to clot. For him, normal boyhood cuts and scrapes could result in severe bleeding, or even death, and so he led a sheltered life. To teach him about the world outside, Duckworth suggested that the prince collect autographs.

Charles helped by sending the young prince letters he had received from George MacDonald and other famous friends, and even a letter from John Tenniel about the illustrations for *Alice.* Prince Leopold's album contains an autograph from Charles: "Believe me, at 1.30 A.M., sleepily but sincerely yours, C. L. Dodgson."

Refreshed from his trip, Charles worked on the sequel to *Alice,* which he now called "Looking-glass House." "I wrote to Tenniel again," he reported in May 1868. "Unless he will undertake it, I am quite at a loss." Finally Tenniel agreed to illustrate the book, but only if he could work on his own schedule.

While waiting, Charles planned a move to larger quarters, the finest in Christ Church. Thanks to *Alice,* he could afford a two-story apartment with an entrance hall, two sitting rooms, two turreted alcoves, two bedrooms, a dressing room, dining room, and scullery.

"There seems a bare possibility," he wrote in his diary, "of my erecting a photographing room on the top [of the building]." This room would save him money and time, as he had for some years been renting a studio in Oxford.

His happy thoughts were interrupted by devastating news. "On the evening of June 21," he wrote later, "it pleased God to take to Himself my dear Father. Even in our sorrow may we be enabled still to say: 'Blessed be His holy Name for ever and ever.'"

Charles hurried to Croft to be with his brothers and sisters and Aunt Lucy. "In those solemn days," wrote Charles later:

> when we used to steal one by one, into the darkened room, to take yet another look at the dear calm face, and to pray for strength, the one feature in the room that I remember was a framed text, illuminated by one of my sisters, "Then they are glad, because they are at rest ; and so [God] bringeth them into the haven where they would be!"

Later Charles called the loss of his father, "The greatest blow that has ever fallen on *my* life," but he quickly assumed his new role as head of the family. He was thirty-six at this time; his youngest brother, Edwin, was twenty-two. Wilfred had left home to seek a living in real estate, but as yet he could not support himself. Skeffington, who had been working as their father's curate, would need a new position. "May God help me to be a real comfort to the dear ones around me!" wrote Charles.

Where to live was the most pressing question, as the family now had to leave the Croft Rectory. The Dodgsons chose to move to Guildford, a small town twenty-five miles southwest of London.

There Charles leased The Chestnuts, a three-story house with eight bedrooms. Arranging for Edwin to take an examination for post office work, Charles also helped Skeffington to find a new curacy.

In September Charles's sister Mary became engaged. Charles wrote to her fiancé, Charles Edward Stuart Collingwood, rector of Southwick and a longtime family friend:

> My dear (future) Brother-in-law,
>   I sincerely rejoice in the news of your engagement, and . . . I pray God to bless you both in your new life. . . . Her [Mary's] letters, breathing as they do a deep real peace and comfort (real because religious) are a great pleasure to me to read.

Mary was the only one of Charles's sisters to marry. He supported the other six for the rest of his life.

Charles "gave Mary away" at her wedding. Nine months later, he wrote to her, "God bless you and the little one now entrusted to you—and may you be to him what our own dear mother was to *her* eldest son!" This nephew, Stuart Dodgson Collingwood, would grow up to write the first biography of Lewis Carroll.

In 1869, a year after agreeing to illustrate the sequel to *Alice,* Tenniel still had not started work. Waiting patiently, Charles published *Phantasmagoria,* a book of humorous poetry for adults. That same year the first translations of *Alice* came out in German and French, with other translations soon to follow. Charles urged translators to adapt songs and poems from their own languages, to make the books more meaningful to child readers.

On June 25, 1870, Charles wrote, a "wonderful thing occurred, Mrs. Liddell brought Lorina and Alice to be photographed." For the last time, he took pictures of his friends, who were now poised young ladies of twenty and eighteen.

Alice Liddell looks sad in Charles's last photograph of her. Charles continued to give Alice and the other Liddells inscribed copies of all his books, including foreign-language editions.

John Tenniel drew Alice going through the looking-glass. The book of the same name ends with an acrostic poem: the first letter of each line, read downward, spells the name Alice Pleasance Liddell.

Chapter Seven

Through the Looking-Glass
1871–1874

I am completely weary of drawing on wood; perfectly sick of wood engraving," wrote artist John Tenniel, after finishing the illustrations for *Through the Looking-Glass and What Alice Found There*. For two years he had worked, making dozens of small changes—in the curl of an eyelash or the shape of a leg—to please Charles. But Tenniel was a perfectionist, too. "Kittens more *fluffy*," he instructed the engravers. "Less like *China*."

Often Tenniel deferred to Charles, but for this book, he objected to a chapter about a wasp in a wig. "Don't think me brutal," he wrote, "but I am bound to say that the 'wasp' character doesn't interest me in the least, & I can't see my way to a picture. If you want to shorten the book, I can't help thinking—with all submission—that there is the opportunity." Charles removed the chapter.

Charles worried most about the book's frontispiece (the illustration facing the title page). Tenniel's drawing of the

Jabberwock, an imaginary beast, seemed too frightening for a children's book. Charles sent copies of this picture to thirty mothers, asking whether to keep it, move it, or discard it. Eventually he moved the Jabberwock illustration to page twenty-three and changed the frontispiece to a picture of Alice and the White Knight.

Through the Looking-Glass, dated 1872 but published in late 1871, was dedicated to Alice Liddell. In this book, the fictional Alice climbs through a huge mirror over the fireplace and emerges into a looking-glass room, the reverse image of her living room. From her new perspective, the room is transformed, with live pictures on the wall and a clock face that grins at her. Finding a book with reversed writing, she holds it up to the mirror to read the poem "Jabberwocky" first seen in *Mischmasch,* Charles's 1855 family magazine.

The plot of *Through the Looking-Glass* is based on the game of chess. Alice makes her way across a checkered landscape, meeting live chess pieces while trying to become a queen. She encounters talking flowers, more exotic than the blossoms the real Alice had seen with Charles in the Botanic Garden, and a little fawn, like those in the deer park in Oxford's Magdalen College. She visits the old Sheep's shop, which Tenniel drew as the reverse image of a real Oxford shop, and she goes rowing on the river.

Mirror images abound, especially the twin brothers Tweedledum and Tweedledee. They tell Alice the story of the Walrus and the Carpenter, who invite a group of young oysters to go for a walk and end by eating them all. Alice meets Humpty Dumpty, who may be a spoof of Oxford professors. "When *I* use a word," he says, in rather a scornful tone, "it means just what I choose it to mean—neither more nor less." She also encounters two Anglo-Saxon messengers (Hatta and

Alice meets Tweedledum and Tweedledee. In this dream country, the visitor, Alice, is sane, and the natives seem mad. Charles may have been commenting on how British travelers felt in foreign lands.

Haigha, who are clearly the Hatter and the March Hare from the first book), and a Lion and a Unicorn.

The White Knight, a comic, clumsy, melancholy old man, escorts Alice for a part of her journey. Although Tenniel drew the White Knight to resemble himself, with a long, drooping moustache, literary critics think that the White Knight's personality represents Charles, bidding farewell to his child-friend as she enters adulthood. Charles wrote:

> Of all the strange things that Alice saw in her journey Through the Looking-Glass, this was the one that she always remembered most clearly. Years afterwards she could bring the whole scene back again, as if it had been only yesterday—the mild blue eyes and kindly smile of the Knight—the setting sun gleaming

through his hair, and shining on his armour in a blaze of light that quite dazzled her.

Alice does become a queen and attends a chaotic dinner. When she can stand it no longer, she rips the cloth off the table, ending her adventure and her dream.

Through the Looking-Glass earned excellent reviews. "It would be difficult," said the *Athenaeum,* "to over-estimate the value of the store of hearty and healthy fun laid up for whole generations of young people by Mr. Lewis Carroll and Mr. John Tenniel in the two books." The *Globe* said, "to write good nonsense is as difficult as to write good sense, but it must be more difficult, as there are very few who deal in the commodity so successfully as Mr. Carroll."

With the book done, Charles turned his attention to activities at Christ Church. Dean Liddell and others planned changes to college buildings, renovations that Charles opposed. "We see the Governing Body," protested Charles, in a squib. "Where is the Governing *Mind?*" Though Students now belonged to the college's governing body, Charles and his associates lacked the votes to prevail, and construction began.

One alteration created a new entrance (nicknamed the Tunnel) to the cathedral. Heavy bells were removed from the cathedral tower, which had become unsafe, and they were housed in an ugly wooden box on the roof of the Hall. In a squib called *The New Belfry,* Charles explained that the bell box had been designed to resemble a gigantic copy of the Greek lexicon, Dean Liddell's famous book. At the next Christ Church banquet, he predicted, each guest would be presented with "a portable model of the new Belfry, tastefully executed in cheese." He named the box the Tea Chest, and a gap beside it he called the Trench.

Usually Dean Liddell ignored Charles's squibs, but the next one made him angry. *The Vision of the Three T's* (Tunnel, Tea Chest, and Trench) described fishing in the pond in Tom Quad. Charles wrote:

> The Commoner kinds [of fish] we may let pass...
> they are so slow, and withal have so little in them, that
> they are good for nothing. . . .
> I will say somewhat of the Nobler kinds, and
> chiefly of the Gold-fish, which is a species highly
> thought of, and much sought after in these parts, not
> only by men, but by divers birds, as for example the
> King-fishers.

Dean Liddell and all of Oxford recognized that "King-fishers" stood for Mrs. Liddell, who was known to be seeking rich, powerful husbands for her daughters. Her first efforts proved successful: in 1874 Lorina married William Baillie Skene, a wealthy young Scotsman.

Meanwhile, Prince Leopold, Queen Victoria's youngest son and Robinson Duckworth's former pupil, had matriculated at Christ Church. Invited often to the Deanery, he and Alice formed an attachment. But the romance was doomed, as Queen Victoria would have found Alice an unsuitable match for her son.

Charles's own family seemed happily settled. Wilfred had found work managing the estates of a wealthy man. In his early thirties, he married his love, Alice Jane Donkin, aged about twenty. Objections overcome, the Dodgsons welcomed her warmly.

At Guildford the sisterhood led happy, busy lives. Mary had a second son. Skeffington, who changed jobs frequently, continued as a curate. Edwin had left the post office to study for the priesthood.

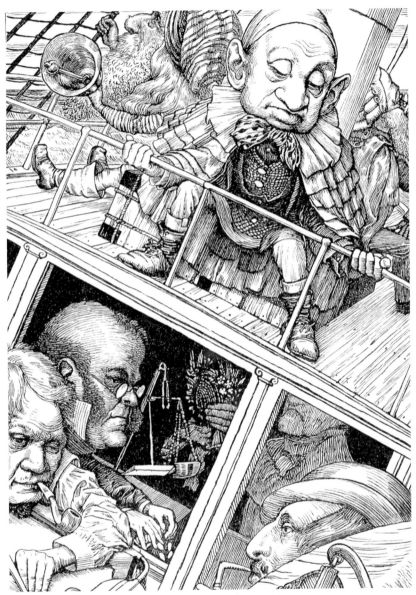

The Crew on Board (illustration by Henry Holiday for The Hunting of the Snark*). Fans of the book formed Snark clubs to stalk the mysterious beast.*

Chapter Eight

The Hunting of the Snark

1874–1880

A number of little girls, bursting with youthful spirits, and all agog for mischief, danced along one of the paths [in the Parks at Oxford], a staid governess bringing up the rear. Presently one of their number spied a tall, black clerical figure in the distance, swinging along towards the little group with a characteristic briskness, almost jerkiness, of step.—"Here comes Mr. Dodgson," she cried. "Let's make a barrier across the path so that he can't pass." No sooner said than done—the children joined hands and formed a line across the path; the clerical figure, appreciating the situation, advanced at the double and charged the line with his umbrella.

Ethel Arnold, one of the girls, told this story many years later. As children, she and her sister Julia were the first subjects to pose for Charles in his new, rooftop studio. With this convenient glass house, he could photograph year-round.

Evelyn Hatch, another child-friend and model, recalled:

climbing up the dark oak staircase leading out of Tom
Quad to the studio. . . . The smell of certain chemicals . . . the mysterious dark cupboard where he developed his plates . . . the dressing-room where
strange costumes had to be donned, and . . . the rather
awe-inspiring ceremony of being posed, with fastidi-
ous care, as Turk, Chinaman, fisher-boy, or in a group
with several others.

To help his young subjects hold still for long poses,
Charles sometimes leaned them on props or supported their
heads with headrests. To amuse them, he collected toys: a
clockwork bear, a rabbit that popped out of a cabbage, music
boxes, and a realistic toy bat. Charles had made the bat himself from wire, black gauze, and a rubber band. It was famous
in Christ Church for having flown out a window, landing on a
servant's tray, and causing a terrific crash.

Evelyn Hatch said:

Boys as well as girls were invited to be photographed,
but opinions were somewhat divided as to whether it
were really a great treat. . . . there is a certain expres-
sion of boredom on the faces of some of his young
models, who remember that the studio was very hot,
and that they used to get very tired of sitting still!
Occasionally, as a reward, they were allowed to go out
to the flat roof above, and look at the view of the
Oxford towers.

Sometimes Charles led his guests up the spiral staircase
to the bell tower over the main entrance to Tom Quad. There
the children could see and touch the seven-ton bell known as
Great Tom. Sometimes Charles let them strike the bell, causing confusion on the ground below, where people wondered
if their watches had stopped.

The summer of 1874 found Charles at The Chestnuts, helping his sister Fanny to nurse their twenty-two-year-old cousin. Charlie Wilcox was suffering from tuberculosis, in those days a fatal disease. After sitting up most of the night with the patient, Charles went out for fresh air. "I was walking on a hillside alone," he wrote:

> when suddenly there came into my head one line of verse—one solitary line—'For the Snark *was* a Boojum, you see.' I knew not what it meant ... but I wrote it down; and, some time afterwards, the rest of the stanza occurred to me, that being its last line: and so by degrees, at odd moments during the next year or two, the rest of the poem pieced itself together.

Sadly, Charlie Wilcox died four months later. Charles's long narrative poem, begun during that trying time, became his book *The Hunting of the Snark.*

Charles worked on *The Snark* during a summer holiday at Sandown, a resort town on the east coast of the Isle of Wight. At the beach, he noticed one particular child who played barefoot, dressed in short pants and a fisherman's jersey. Eight-year-old Gertrude Chataway stood out from the other beachgoers, who strolled on the sand fully dressed.

Gertrude, whose family was staying next door to Charles, rushed outside whenever she heard the "old gentleman's" footstep. After a few days, he spoke to her, asking, "Little girl, why do you come so fast on to your balcony whenever I come out?"

"To see you sniff," she said. "It is lovely to see you sniff like this," and she threw her head back and breathed in deeply.

Soon Charles met her parents and three sisters. Gertrude remembered, "We used to sit for hours on the wooden steps which led from our garden on to the beach, whilst he told me the most lovely tales. . . . One thing that made his stories so particularly charming for a child was that he often took his cue from her remarks." Charles told Gertrude stories about his fairy characters, Sylvie and Bruno, and recited verses for her from *The Hunting of the Snark.*

To illustrate *The Snark*, Charles chose Henry Holiday, a painter and designer of stained glass windows. The two men had been friends for some years.

Charles sometimes used Holiday's house as a London base for photography, and Holiday had visited Charles at Christ Church. There Holiday had helped to pose a new model, Alexandra Kitchin, who was nicknamed X or Xie (pronounced Ehk-see). After Alice Liddell, Xie, who had been born in 1864, became Charles's most important model.

Holiday collected Charles's photographs of Xie as they

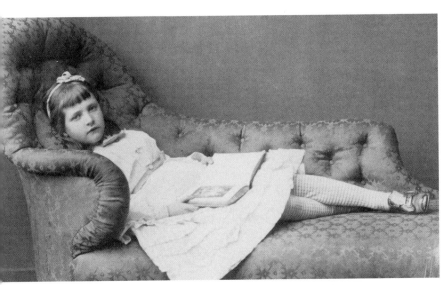

Charles took this picture of Xie Kitchin in 1872. He told Henry Holiday how to obtain excellence in a photograph: "Take a lens and put Xie before it." (A play on the word excellence—X a lens.)

worked together on *The Hunting of the Snark.* As usual, Charles supervised his illustrator closely. One drawing, of the imaginary creature called the Boojum, Charles rejected entirely.

"Mr Dodgson wrote that it was a delightful monster," recalled Holiday later, "but that it was inadmissible. All his descriptions of the Boojum were quite unimaginable, and he wanted the creature to remain so."

The book begins:

"JUST the place for a Snark!" the Bellman cried,
As he landed his crew with care;
Supporting each man on the top of the tide
By a finger entwined in his hair.

"Just the place for a Snark! I have said it twice:
That alone should encourage the crew.
"Just the place for a Snark! I have said it thrice:
What I tell you three times is true."

Besides the Bellman, the crew consists of a Boots (a hotel servant who cleaned boots), Bonnet-maker, Barrister, Broker, Billiard-marker, Banker, Beaver, Baker, and Butcher. Holiday said, "I asked Lewis Carroll when first I read his M.S. [manuscript] why he made all the members of the crew have occupations beginning with B."

"Why not?" replied Charles.

The plot centers on a hunt for a mythical creature, the Snark.

THEY sought it with thimbles, they sought it with care;
They pursued it with forks and hope;
They threatened its life with a railway-share;
They charmed it with smiles and soap.

The Hunting of the Snark, dedicated to Gertrude Chataway,

was published in 1876. Though reviews were poor, the book intrigued many readers and sold well. "Some children are puzzled with it," wrote Charles to a young friend. "Of course you know what a Snark is? if you do, please tell *me*: for I haven't an idea of what it was like."

His fun was disrupted by tragic news. "I have had a great sorrow to bear," he wrote to Gertrude Chataway's mother:

> ... in hearing of the sudden death of the third daugh-
> ter of the Dean of Christ Church (one of the three I
> think I have told you of—the most intimate child-
> friends I ever had), just one week after she had been
> engaged to be married, and when life must have been
> at its brightest. But the world, even at its brightest, is
> not worthy to be compared with the glory that shall
> be revealed.

Edith Liddell, aged twenty-two, had died of peritonitis, a fatal infection in the days before antibiotics. Six months later, Mrs. Liddell called on Charles to see his photographs of Edith, and she accepted several as gifts.

In the meantime, Charles had found a new summer home on the south coast of England, at Eastbourne. Number 7 Lushington Road became Charles's holiday lodging for nineteen years. Mrs. Dyer, the landlady, rented him a sitting room with a balcony, and a bedroom on the floor above.

At Eastbourne, Charles met the Hulls—a mother, lawyer father, four daughters, and a son. Agnes, aged ten, became his favorite. In London he took her to see Ellen Terry in a play at the Lyceum Theatre.

By this time, Ellen Terry was the foremost actress on the British stage. Charles had broken off their friendship for twelve years because of her shocking personal life. While still married to her first husband, who had abandoned her, she began living

Ellen Terry, photographed by Charles at her parents' London home near the time of their first meeting in 1865.

with an architect, Edward Godwin, and had two children with him. Charles, though sympathetic, could not approve.

After separating from Godwin, Ellen Terry finally had been divorced by her husband. On stage her career soared, but her status as a "fallen woman" with two "illegitimate" children limited her friendships to a liberal group of artists, writers, and actors, not including Charles. For herself, the actress did not mind being ostracized, but she worried about her daughter and son.

In 1878 she married actor Charles Wardell and became more respectable in the eyes of society. Contacting her through her mother, Charles soon called on Mrs. Wardell. "She was as charming as ever," he wrote, "and I was much pleased with her husband. . . . I also liked her two children, Edith and Eddie."

In the years to come, Ellen Terry proved generous to Charles and his friends. For Agnes Hull, Charles had requested an autographed book from the actress. A messenger delivered it to their seats at intermission, with a bouquet of violets, which Agnes declared she would keep for the rest of her life.

In 1879 Charles met the London artist Emily Gertrude Thomson, aged twenty-nine. After admiring her drawings of nude fairies, he had written to her in care of her publisher.

"Soon after our meeting, " said Thomson later, "he wrote from Oxford: 'Are you sufficiently unconventional (I *think* you are) to defy Mrs. Grundy and come down to spend the day with me at Oxford? Write and ask permission of your father.'"

"To defy Mrs. Grundy" was a slang term, meaning to break the rules governing social behavior. In Victorian England, middle-class, unmarried women under the age of thirty needed permission from their parents to make social engagements. Women did not usually visit men unchaperoned either, but Charles felt that such visits were acceptable if the father approved. Thomson's father granted his permission, and the visit, the first of many, was arranged.

Taking photographs and sketching together, Charles and Gertrude Thomson became friends. Some believe that she fell in love with Charles, who was forty-seven at this time. But even though the rules at Christ Church had changed in 1878, allowing dons (the teaching staff) to marry, Charles considered himself a confirmed old bachelor. Nevertheless, his friendship with Gertrude Thomson and his occasional nude photographic studies were beginning to cause talk in Oxford.

It is important to remember that nude studies, especially of children, were popular subjects for artists and photographers. In the male-dominated Victorian society, children, especially girls—clothed or nude—symbolized purity and innocence. Their pretty pictures were everywhere: in advertisements, on greeting cards, and in the work of serious artists and photographers.

Charles first recorded photographing a nude on May 27,

1867. He wrote in his journal, "Mrs. Latham brought Beatrice, and I took photographs of the two; and several of Beatrice alone, *sans habilement* [French for "without clothes"]."

Over the years, he continued to make nude studies. On July 18, 1879, he wrote: "Mrs. Henderson brought Annie and Frances [to be photographed]. I . . . was especially surprised to find they were ready for any amount of undress, and seemed delighted at being allowed to run about naked."

When photographing children, Charles always obtained permission. Usually he had another adult present; most often the subject's mother. Gertrude Thomson helped him to photograph the Hendersons. With nude studies, Charles took special care, destroying negatives and sealing prints into envelopes with instructions to burn them, unopened, upon his death.

Recently, much attention has been focused on Charles's nude studies, even though these amount to less than 1 percent of all the pictures he took. Only six such prints, two of boys and four of girls, have survived to the present day.

One of these photographs shows the Henderson sisters. Charles sent a copy to their mother. It had been hand-painted by an artist who added bits of cloth for modesty and a shipwreck in the background. "I hope you will like this," he wrote, adding, "Love to the two Misses Robinson Crusoe."

Though Charles felt sorry that gossip about his pictures might hurt his friends' feelings, he was convinced that his own actions were proper. "On no account," he wrote to the mother of a young subject, "would I do a picture which I should be unwilling to show to all the world—or at least all the artistic world."

To his cousin Lucy Wilcox he wrote, "As some folk are said to 'live on the smiles of Fortune,' so may *I* be said to live on the frowns of Mrs. Grundy."

The first professional stage production based on the Alice books opened in London in 1886. "Phoebe Carlo is a splendid Alice," wrote Charles, after seeing it. "And little Dorothy d'Alcourt ([aged] 6 ½) a delicious dormouse."

(hapter Nine

An Animal That Writes Letters

1880–1887

In July 1880, Charles packed his photographic equipment and left it, as he always did, at Christ Church, while he went to the seashore. He never used it again. One year later, he called photography "a very tiring amusement." No photographic subject, he said, was "tempting enough to make me face the labor of getting the studio in order again."

He may have given up photography to devote more time to writing. In his late forties, Charles worried that he would not live long enough to complete all the writing projects he had planned. Decreasing his teaching hours, he suggested that the college cut his pay, and his offer was accepted.

Changes in his personal life may have made him feel older. On September 3, Charles's sister Fanny telegraphed for him to come at once to Guildford, where Aunt Lucy lay critically ill. Charles arrived in time to see his dear aunt die, "with us all round her."

Later that month, Alice Liddell married Reginald Hargreaves, a wealthy young graduate of Christ Church. Charles and his friend Thomas Vere Bayne sent the couple a watercolor of Tom Quad as a wedding present.

And to Charles's surprise, his brother Skeffington also married. "He had kept it all a secret," wrote Charles, "and I am thankful to have no responsibility."

Wilfred, who had eight children by this time, was well established, but their youngest brother Edwin still worried Charles. In 1881 Edwin, now a missionary, sailed for Tristan da Cunha, a small island off the west coast of southern Africa. His congregation, the entire population of the island, numbered 107.

"I cannot think he will find this an object worthy to devote much of his life to—" wrote Charles, "with so many thousands in equal need in England."

Charles worried more when he got a letter from the island. The local economy, Edwin wrote, had depended on selling fresh meat and vegetables to passing ships. Overhunting had depleted huge schools of whales and seals, so ships no longer called. The islanders survived by growing wheat and eating wild potatoes.

Charles stayed in close touch with his brother and with many friends and relatives by writing thousands of letters. Standing for hours at a tall desk, using purple ink, he filled page after page with his neat handwriting.

His most charming letters were to children, like this one to Mary MacDonald:

> My Dear Mary,
> Once upon a time there was a little girl, and she had a cross old Uncle . . . and this little girl had promised to copy out for him a sonnet Mr. Rosetti had

written about Shakespeare. Well, and she didn't do it, you know: and the poor old Uncle's nose kept getting longer and longer, and his temper getting shorter and shorter, and post after post went by, and no sonnet came—I leave off here to explain how they sent letters in those days: there were no gates, so the gate-posts weren't obliged to stay in one place—consequence of which, they went wandering all over the country—consequence of which, if you wanted to send a letter anywhere, all you had to do was to fasten it on to a gate-post that was going in the proper direction (only they sometimes changed their minds, which was awkward). This was called "sending a letter by the post." They did things very simply in those days: if you had a lot of money, you just dug a hole under the hedge, and popped it in: and then you said you had "put it in the bank," and you felt quite comfortable about it. And the way they travelled was— there were railings all along the side of the road, and they used to get up, and walk along the top, as steadily as they could, till they tumbled off—which they mostly did very soon. This was called "travelling by rail." Now to return to the wicked little girl. The end of her was, that a great black WOLF came, and—I don't like to go on, but nothing was found of her afterwards except 3 small bones.
    I make no remark. It is rather a horrid story.
    Your loving friend,
    C. L. Dodgson

Many of Charles's letters were illustrated. "*Please* don't grow any taller, if you can help it, till I've had time to photograph you again," he wrote to Xie Kitchin, adding a sketch of a carte de visite. "Cartes like this (it always happens if people get too tall) never really look nice." In his drawing, her head is cut off at the top of the card.

    Some letters were written backward, beginning with "CLD, Uncle loving your" and ending with "Nelly dear my."

Charles was a shrewd businessman who designed an Alice stamp case and approved a biscuit tin with Alice pictures. Marketing toys with books was unusual in his lifetime.

Or he reversed his handwriting, so that the recipient, like Alice in *Through the Looking-Glass,* had to view the letter in a mirror in order to read it. Often Charles sent acrostic poems, in which the first letter of each line spelled the recipient's name. Some verse he disguised as prose to see whether the reader would notice. His writing appeared sometimes as a spiral or a rebus, with drawings substituted for words. Tiny letters, supposedly from fairies, were written with a special pen on tiny paper, to be read with a magnifying glass.

Charles received many letters from fans. Though he often answered mail sent to Lewis Carroll in care of his publisher, he refused letters addressed to that name at Christ

Church. In time he developed a "Stranger Circular," a form letter, which said:

> Mr Dodgson . . . neither claims nor acknowledges any connection with any pseudonym, or with any book that is not published under his own name. Having therefore no claim to retain, or even to read the enclosed [letter], he returns it for the convenience of the writer who has thus misaddressed it.

When Charles wrote a letter, he began with a first draft, then wrote a good copy to send, and a third copy to file. In a numerical register, begun in 1861, he recorded and indexed each letter. "Life seems to go in letter-writing," he wrote to Marion Terry, Ellen's younger sister, "and I'm beginning to think that the proper definition of 'Man' is 'an animal that writes letters.'"

On October 18, 1881, Charles resigned his mathematical lectureship altogether. "There is a sadness in coming to the end of anything in Life," he wrote. "Man's instincts cling to the Life that will never end." He retained his Studentship, his residence in Tom Quad, and voting power in Christ Church and Oxford University.

A year later, Charles took on a new role at the college when he was elected curator, or honorary steward, of the Common Room. The curator ran this social club for his fellow graduates of Christ Church. "It will take me out of myself a little," wrote Charles, of the position.

The Common Room's four rooms provided a congenial setting where men could socialize. The curator ordered food, wines, coal, newspapers, stationery, and furniture, and hired the Common Room servants. Charles pleased his colleagues by installing a wine cellar and a smoking room (he did not smoke) and by writing humorous pamphlets about his work:

> A Curator who contents himself with simply *doing* the business of the Common Room and puts out no statistics, is sure to be distrusted. "He keeps us in the dark!" men will say. "He publishes no figures. What does it mean? Is he assisting himself?" But, only circulate some abstruse tables of figures, particularly if printed in lines and columns, so that ordinary readers can make nothing of them, and all is changed at once. "Oh, go on, go on!'" they say, satiated with facts. "Manage things as you like! We trust you entirely."

Helping others gave Charles great satisfaction, but some problems could not be solved. Edwin wrote of worsening conditions on Tristan da Cunha. A shipwreck had released dozens of rats onto the island. Soon rats swarmed everywhere, eating crops, grass, and even the interiors of houses. The demoralized islanders were near starvation.

Charles suggested moving the entire population to a better location, such as South Africa. With Edwin's approval, he took this idea to London, calling on church leaders and government officials. Though some financial aid was sent, the islanders were not moved. After four years, with no solution found, Edwin fell ill and returned to live with his sisters at The Chestnuts.

At age fifty-three, Charles seemed busier than ever. "Never before have I had so many literary projects on hand at once," he wrote. In his journal he listed fifteen. Three of these were books for children.

For a picture book, *The Nursery Alice,* Charles wrote a simplified text for younger children, and John Tenniel created twenty new, colored illustrations. Charles asked Gertrude Thomson to do the cover art.

A second project involved the real Alice, now Alice Hargreaves, the mother of two sons. Charles wrote to her:

MY DEAR MRS. HARGREAVES,—I fancy this will come to you almost like a voice from the dead, after so many years of silence, and yet those years have made no difference . . . my mental picture is as vivid as ever, of one who was, through so many years, my ideal child-friend. I have had scores of child-friends since your time: but they have been quite a different thing.

. . . Would you have any objection to the original MS. book of "Alice's Adventures" . . . being published in facsimile? . . . I would be much obliged if you would lend it me . . . I have not seen it for about twenty years, so am by no means sure that the illustrations may not prove to be so awfully bad, that to reproduce them would be absurd.

Gertrude Thomson's cover art for The Nursery "Alice"

Alice agreed to the plan, and Charles's original illustrations were not so bad as he had feared. He donated profits from the facsimile book to children's hospitals.

The third idea grew into a long, two-volume novel. *Sylvie and Bruno* began as fairy tales told to child-friends over a twenty-year period. They grew into a confusing and preachy story. Reviews and sales proved disappointing, but Charles moved forward with new efforts.

For years Charles had tried to bring *Alice* to the stage. He had copyrighted the dialogue from both books in play format, to prevent other writers from adapting his work. In 1867 he had proposed *Alice* as a pantomime. In 1877 he had discussed with composer Arthur Sullivan the possibility of an *Alice* operetta, but nothing came of either idea. On September 2, 1886, he wrote in his journal of a dream coming true:

> I got an application from Mr. H. Savile Clarke, for leave to make a two act Operetta out of *Alice* and *Looking-Glass*. I have written my consent, on condition of "no *suggestion* even of coarseness in libretto or in stage business."

As Charles waited eagerly for the Savile Clarke show to be developed, he worked on a textbook on logic. At a girls' high school and college in Oxford, he gave lectures on the same topic. His child-friend Evelyn Hatch recalled how a dozen girls:

> assembled solemnly in the library, armed with notebooks and pencils, prepared to listen to a serious lecture on a difficult subject. To their surprise, and also somewhat to their dismay, Mr. Dodgson produced from his black bag twelve large white envelopes, each containing a card marked with a diagram, and a set of

counters in two colours. These he dealt out to his audience. "Now," he said cheerfully, "I will teach you to play the game of Logic!" And then, when he proceeded to illustrate his explanations with examples, his pupils found that they were actually expected to *laugh!*

Lecturing convinced Charles to publish *The Game of Logic,* a book of practical examples to accompany his text. Like the Oxford girls, readers were charmed by Charles's propositions, such as

No bald person needs a hair-brush;
No lizards have hair;
[Therefore] no lizard needs a hair-brush.

On December 23, 1886, *Alice in Wonderland* opened in London at the Prince of Wales' Theatre. "A tolerably eventful week for me!" wrote Charles.

He had maintained close control over the play, writing ninety-seven letters to the producers in a span of four months. Although he liked the show, after seeing it, he wrote a ninety-eighth letter, offering improvements in the finale. Soon he had written a new ending, bringing in the ghosts of three oysters. The ghosts get revenge for having been eaten by sitting on the Carpenter and stamping on the Walrus's chest.

A month later, Charles returned to the play. "The oyster-ghosts are a great addition," he wrote, proud that the audience had applauded his new characters.

This portrait of Charles in old age was painted after his death by Sir Hubert von Herkomer.

Chapter Ten

Their Watchful Uncle

1887–1898

Four of my (seven) sisters are here," Charles wrote to a friend from their home in Guildford, "and there is, as you may imagine, *some* conversation going on. In fact, I get such a supply of it here, that I am content to spend *weeks* of silence when I get back to Oxford!" Charles spent holidays with his sisters. Sometimes when the family gathered, the house became so crowded that he moved to a nearby inn. Wilfred's daughter Menella recalled a childhood visit to The Chestnuts, "standing on a drawing-room sofa on arrival and being kissed by what seemed an endless succession of aunts all exactly alike."

Charles enjoyed his young relatives. Asking Wilfred to notify him when his nieces and nephews were old enough to be given watches, Charles wrote, "I would like to earn the character, among your children, of 'our *watchful* Uncle.'"

When Wilfred's daughter Violet was thirteen, she visited her uncle on the coast in Eastbourne for "ten days so crowded with good things that I had no time to feel lost or homesick."

"He took me to my first real theatre," wrote Menella, of a play starring Ellen Terry's sister Marion, "and I came away dazed with the glamour of it all."

Not all Victorian children lived such happy lives as Charles's young relatives. In the late 1880s, British politicians began to consider the issue of crimes against children. The very idea was a new concept in a society where children and women had few rights. Newspaper stories about child prostitution led to passage of a new law, raising the age of consent for sexual activity for girls from thirteen to sixteen.

Some reformers focused on child actors, attempting to ban them from working on the stage. Charles objected, pointing out in letters to newspapers that the theater offered one of the few respectable sources of income available to young women. His suggestions, to limit children's work and require them to pass examinations, proved very close to the regulations that were finally adopted.

The controversy was being discussed as a touring company of the *Alice* operetta played at Brighton, near Eastbourne. Charles gave books to the forty-one children in the cast, but one girl, who had a bit part, interested him especially. Isabella (Isa) Bowman, aged thirteen, was the eldest child of a theatrical family.

In October 1887, Charles brought Isa to Eastbourne for a week. They went for long walks together, and he read the Bible with her, taught her geometry, and took her to see the Wild West Show starring Buffalo Bill.

Charles invited many relatives and child-friends to Eastbourne. The landlady, Mrs. Dyer, housed Charles's guests, like Violet and Isa, in a separate room and served as a chaperone. When his sisters were there, they helped him to entertain. As Charles grew older, his definition of a child-friend expanded to include older girls in their teens and even young women in their twenties. He took special pleasure in inviting girls from theatrical families, who could not otherwise have afforded trips to the seashore. Tactfully, Charles paid his guests' train fares, showed them the sights, bought them books, shoes, and clothes, and even took them to the dentist or doctor. For Isa and her younger sister Nellie, he hired a French tutor. Knowing that producer Henry Savile Clarke planned to restage *Alice* in London, Charles suggested Isa as the new lead.

On January 3, 1889, Charles attended the new *Alice* play. "Isa makes a delightful 'Alice,' " he wrote, "and Emsie [another of Isa's sisters] is wonderfully good as 'Dormouse'. . . Charlie [their brother] is 'White Rabbit.' "

Later, Charles arranged for Isa to have singing lessons, and he asked Ellen Terry to recommend an elocution (public speaking) teacher for her. When the famous actress offered to coach Isa herself, Charles was thrilled. "You really are too nice and kind for anything!" he wrote to her. "And so you have found out that secret—one of the deep secrets of Life—that all, that is really worth the doing, is what we do for others?"

Helping young friends gave Charles great pleasure, though his actions were sometimes criticized. After Gertrude Chataway, by this time a young woman in her twenties, visited at Eastbourne, Charles's sister Mary Collingwood wrote to warn him that people were talking.

Charles replied:

> I think all you say about my girl-guests is most kind and sisterly. . . . You and your husband have, I think, been very fortunate to know so little . . . of the wicked recklessness with which people repeat things to the disadvantage of others, without a thought as to

whether they have grounds for asserting what they say. I have met with a good deal of utter misrepresentation of that kind. . . . The only two tests I now apply to such a question as the having some particular girl-friend as a guest are, first, my own *conscience,* to settle whether I feel it to be entirely innocent and right, in the sight of God; secondly, the *parents* of my friend, to settle whether I have their *full* approval of what I do. . . . If you limit your actions in life to things that *nobody* can possibly find fault with, you will not do much!

In 1896 Wilfred and his wife decided to send their daughters to the High School at Oxford. Violet, Beatrice, and Gladys arrived by train. "From the moment when [Uncle Charles] met us at the station," Violet recalled later

he took us under his wing and ran round after us like a hen fussing over her chicks. He showed us Oxford, introduced us to his friends . . . made us free of his

Charles's sitting room had green wallpaper, red curtains, and a red sofa and chair covers. The fireplace tiles, with pictures of strange beasts, represented characters from his books.

rooms at Christ Church, saw to it that we had everything we needed, friends, amusements, books. . . . We
used to find little notes awaiting us after school.

As an undergraduate at Christ Church, Mary's son Stuart
Collingwood received many invitations from Charles. On July
1, 1891, Charles reported the "Arrival of a host of enthusiastic
relatives to see Stuart Collingwood take his B.A. tomorrow."

Though Charles enjoyed visits with family, he curtailed
other social events. "My objection to parties (and most visits)," he wrote to a friend, "is the *utter* waste of time and brain
in talking perfectly useless small-talk."

In November 1891, Mrs. Liddell invited him to a
Deanery reception for the Duchess of Albany. The duchess
was the widow of Prince Leopold, Alice Liddell's former love.
Leopold had died in 1884 from a stroke. The duchess's visit
took place when Dean Liddell had just announced his retire-
ment and his plans to move. Declining the invitation, Charles
wrote to Mrs. Liddell:

> It seems but yesterday when the Dean, and you, first
> arrived: yet I was hardly more than a boy, then; and
> many of the pleasantest memories of those early
> years . . . are bound up with the names of yourself and
> your children: and now I am an old man, already be-
> ginning to feel a little weary of life—at any rate weary
> of its *pleasures,* and only caring to go on, on the chance
> of doing a little more *work.*

Though he did not want to attend the reception, Charles
was delighted when the visiting duchess sent her children,
Princess Alice and Prince Charlie, to call on him. Charles
taught his young visitors to fold paper pistols that went off
with a bang.

He was always pleased to entertain the Liddells. Over the next few weeks, Rhoda and Violet, the youngest sisters, came for tea, followed by a visit from Mrs. Liddell and Mrs. Skene (Lorina).

Learning that Alice was visiting the Deanery, he invited her to visit, too. "If your husband is here he would be . . . very welcome," wrote Charles. "I met him in our Common Room not long ago. It was hard to realise that he was the husband of one I can scarcely picture myself, even now, as more than 7 years old!" Alice called with Rhoda for an afternoon visit, the last time Charles ever saw her.

Charles retired as curator of the Common Room in 1892, when he was sixty. As he withdrew from university work and parties, he grew more active in the Church, preaching at Oxford, Guildford, and Eastbourne. He still dreaded his speech impediment. "No one, I think," he said, "can understand without experience what a drawback in life hesitation sometimes is."

In 1895 Isa Bowman, aged about twenty-one, visited Oxford as the star of a touring play. Calling on Charles at Christ Church, she told him that she was engaged. The news, she recalled later, seemed to upset him.

"You know I can't stand flowers!" he exclaimed, snatching a little bouquet of roses from her belt and flinging them out the window. But the next day, he gave a dinner party in his rooms for Isa and her fiancé.

The first volume of Charles's book *Symbolic Logic,* intended for young people, was published in 1896. Reviews were good. Though Charles had taught logic to girls, and though he favored higher education for women, he did not think that they belonged at Oxford University. In 1896 the governing body, which included Charles, voted down a proposal to admit women. In a pamphlet, Charles argued that accepting women would overwhelm the university's resources and cause chaos, diminishing the quality of an Oxford education. Instead, he proposed the creation of a women's university.

Having sisters made Charles aware of female ambitions and capabilities. When the youngest, Henrietta, decided to move to Brighton and to live there alone, he supported her decision, even though it was unusual for the time.

At age sixty-five, Charles had white hair and a "fresh, youngish face." Strong and fit, he could stand for ten hours, writing at his desk. Sometimes he rode a velociman, a large tricycle, around the outskirts of Oxford or worked his muscles with a device called a Whiteley Exerciser. In July 1897, he walked twenty miles between Eastbourne and Hastings. "I was hardly at all tired," he reported proudly, "and not at all foot sore."

As usual, he spent Christmas that year at The Chestnuts. Suffering from a cold, he grew too hoarse to lead the customary family prayers.

On January 5, 1898, a telegram arrived from his sister Mary, asking him to come at once to Yorkshire. Her husband, Charles Collingwood, had died suddenly. Charles wrote:

> Dearest Mary,
>   You know, better than I can say it, all that my heart feels for you in your irreparable loss. And you know, better than I can tell you, where to go for strength, and guidance, and, in God's good time, comfort and peace. I would certainly have come to you, if I could have done so with reasonable prudence: but, with a feverish cold, of the bronchial type, . . . Dr. Gabb forbids me to risk it.

I am so glad to think you have two sons to help and comfort. Please give them my love and deep sympathy.

You will very likely be in need of some ready money: so I enclose £50 "on account."

Your loving brother,

C. L. Dodgson

Soon his cold worsened, turning to pneumonia. In those days, the disease was often fatal, but Charles did not fear death. He had written, "I sometimes think what a grand thing it will be to be able to say to oneself, 'Death is *over* now; there is not *that* experience to be faced again.'" He looked forward to a new life after death, with God.

As days passed, his condition declined. Lovingly, his sisters nursed him at The Chestnuts. They sat with him, propping him on pillows to help as he gasped for air.

On January 13, Charles told them, "Take away those pillows, I shall need them no more."

The next day, January 14, 1898, his struggle for breath grew even harder, until one of his sisters heard it stop altogether. The doctor, who had visited Charles regularly, was summoned, but there was nothing more he could do. "How wonderfully young your brother looks!" said the doctor, returning from the upstairs bedroom where Charles's body lay, speaking to the family gathered below.

Charles's will requested a quiet funeral. Gertrude Thomson attended the service, which was held at Saint Mary's Church, Guildford. She described:

A grey January day, calm, and without sound, full of the peace of God which passeth all understanding.

A steep, stony, country road, with hedges close on either side. . . .

A few mourners slowly climbed the hills in silence, while borne before them on a simple hand-bier was the coffin, half hid in flowers.

Under the old yew, round whose gnarled trunk the green ivy twined, in the pure white chalk earth his body was laid to rest, while the slow bell tolled the passing

"Of the sweetest soul
That ever looked with human eyes."

Many of Charles's child-friends sent wreaths for his grave. One came from Alice Hargreaves.

This stained glass panel is in All Saints' Church in Daresbury, England, the village where Charles was born.

Alice Hargreaves arrives in New York in April 1932 to attend the Lewis Carroll Centenary Celebration at Columbia University.

Epilogue

Curiouser and Curiouser

1898–PRESENT

We regret to announce the death of the Rev Charles Lutwidge Dodgson, better known as 'Lewis Carroll'," wrote the London *Times.* The obituary said:

> It is curious to note how frequently *Alice in Wonderland* is quoted in reference to public affairs, as well as to the ordinary matters of everyday life. Hardly a week passes without the employment of its whimsicalities to point a moral or adorn a tale.

Audrey Fuller, a fourteen-year-old child-friend, wrote to the *St. James's Gazette,* proposing a collection to fund an *Alice in Wonderland* bed in the Children's Hospital, in memory of Charles. Donations poured in from Charles's family, Alice Hargreaves, Robinson Duckworth, George MacDonald, Sir John Tenniel (who had been knighted in 1893), Princess Alice, and many others, including fans who had never met their favorite author.

Charles's will divided his assets equally among his siblings. Wilfred went to Christ Church to close Charles's apartment.

Choosing quickly, he saved Charles's diaries, his letter register, some family photographs, and thousands of letters. Someone, probably Wilfred, burned cartloads of papers. What remained of Charles's possessions—his furniture, games, paintings, clocks, opera glasses, dumbbells, Nyctograph (his own invention, used for writing in the dark), and three thousand books—Wilfred sold at auction for £729.

The papers Wilfred kept were given first to his sister Mary's son, Stuart Collingwood, for use in writing *The Life and Letters of Lewis Carroll*. In this book, Collingwood portrayed his uncle as an eccentric clergyman who loved little girls. To Charles's family, this characterization cast their famous relative in the best possible light. It created the mythical portrait of Charles that has endured.

The Dodgsons preferred to downplay Charles's more controversial (at that time) affection for older girls and his friendships with mature women. Charles himself had begun to create the myth by using the term "child-friend" for a young female friend, regardless of age, and by complaining about boys even though he did sometimes befriend boys, too.

As Charles had done, the Dodgsons shunned publicity. Content with Collingwood's biography, the family closed ranks, keeping Charles's papers to themselves for half a century.

Several of Charles's child-friends published memoirs of happy times with him. Isa Bowman's book, *The Story of Lewis Carroll, by the Real Alice in Wonderland* (1899), emphasized his love for children. Her account of the friendship between the "little girl and the grave professor" when she was "no more than ten or eleven years old," ignored the fact that she was thirteen when they met. She visited him until she was almost twenty. She may have altered the facts to protect her own reputation, as well as Charles's.

For many years Charles's favorite child-friend, Alice Hargreaves, declined public comment. Saddened by the loss of two sons in World War I (1914–1918), she lived quietly with her husband in the south of England. Both doted on Caryl, their remaining son. Alice's husband died in 1926, when Alice was seventy-three, leaving Caryl short of money to maintain their large home.

To supplement the family income, Alice auctioned her illustrated manuscript of *Alice's Adventures under Ground.* An American book dealer, Dr. A. S. W. Rosenbach, paid £15,400 for it, outbidding the British Museum. This price was the highest ever paid for a literary manuscript.

In 1932 the one hundredth anniversary of Charles's birth rekindled interest in Lewis Carroll. At the urging of her son, Alice, aged eighty, published, for the first time, accounts of her friendship with Mr. Dodgson. She also accepted an invitation to a centennial celebration at Columbia University in New York City. There she received the honorary degree of Doctor of Literature, for inspiring the *Alice* books. She died in England in 1934.

During the centennial celebrations, a new biography of Charles appeared. Its author, Langford Reed, claimed that friendships with young girls were the only emotional outlets in Charles's life, and that Charles had rejected relationships with grown women.

In 1933 Anthony Goldschmidt, an Oxford student, published an article, "Alice in Wonderland Psycho-Analysed." The title reflected a change in society's thinking. Psychoanalysis, a new model of understanding human behavior, described people's actions in terms of disorders that needed curing. The most influential psychoanalyst, Sigmund Freud, taught that people of all ages had sexual needs and that emotional disorders stemmed from problems in handling sexual urges.

By these new standards, little girls were no longer innocent beings; a man who loved little girls exclusively was *not* pure and good. Though Goldschmidt probably intended his article as a parody, other writers soon developed new, sexual interpretations of Charles's books.

In 1933 the first collection of Charles's letters was published, lovingly edited by his former child-friend and photographic subject Evelyn Hatch. The next major biography of Charles, *The Life of Lewis Carroll (Victoria Through the Looking-Glass)*, by Florence Becker Lennon, was published in 1945. Lennon and later biographers added a new theory: that Alice had been the great love of Charles's life, and that he had never recovered from losing her.

As interest grew in Charles's work, Luther H. Evans, United States Librarian of Congress, decided that Alice's handwritten manuscript belonged in England. Raising $50,000 to buy it, he presented it in 1948 to the British Museum, a gift from the United States to the British people, in appreciation for their gallantry in World War II (1939–1945).

A year later, Helmut Gernsheim published his book *Lewis Carroll, Photographer.* Its sixty-four photographs helped to establish Charles as the most outstanding photographer of children from the nineteenth century. Gernsheim described Charles's nude studies, but no examples appeared in the book.

In 1951 Walt Disney released his animated film, *Alice in Wonderland.* (The first *Alice* film, a silent movie, had been made in 1903.) New films, television programs, and plays are still being produced. Around the world, the Disney film continues to motivate new generations to rediscover the books that inspired it.

By the 1950s, ownership of Charles's papers had passed to his niece Menella Dodgson. She agreed to publish excerpts from Charles's diary. As editor Roger Lancelyn Green worked on the project, he discovered that four of the thirteen volumes had been "lost," and that ten pages had been cut from the remaining journals.

Martin Gardner's book *The Annotated Alice* appeared in 1960. Gardner reproduced the text and illustrations to both *Alice* stories, adding helpful notes on background and references. This book made *Alice* accessible and understandable to new audiences.

After Menella Dodgson died in the 1960s, the grandchildren of Charles's siblings inherited his papers. They sold the remaining diaries to the British Museum.

More than fifty years after it was made, Disney's Alice *remains the most influential film version of Charles's work.*

Drug use in the 1960s sparked new interpretations of the *Alice* books and led to essays like *Lewis Carroll—The First Acidhead.* Hookahs, like the Caterpillar's in *Alice's Adventures in Wonderland,* became popular with drug users. Grace Slick's song "White Rabbit" used images from the book to portray the effects of drugs:

> One pill makes you larger,
> And one pill makes you small.
> And the ones that Mother gives you
> Don't do anything at all.
> Go ask Alice
> When she's ten feet tall. . . .

Charles, who was well read on medical topics, certainly knew about drug use, legal and illegal, in his lifetime. But he did not abuse drugs nor did he try to make drugs seem attractive to children.

In 1969 author Anne Clark called the first meeting of the Lewis Carroll Society in England. This organization is still thriving, holding conferences, and publishing original research, including an unabridged, annotated edition of Charles's diaries, edited by Edward Wakeling. The Lewis Carroll Society of North America was founded in 1974, and sister groups meet in Australia, Canada, Holland, Japan, and other countries.

In the 1970s, Professor Morton N. Cohen found four of Charles's photographs of nude girls in the Rosenbach Collection in Philadelphia. In one of these, Evelyn Hatch, undressed, lies facing the camera. This picture, and the thought that there may have been others like it, have made Charles a controversial figure by contemporary standards. Two nude studies of boys have, by contrast, been largely ignored.

In recent years, biographers and critics have concentrated

on details of Charles's life and his friendships with young girls. Unlike earlier research, these studies have been based on original sources, such as his letters and journals.

Charles Lutwidge Dodgson's life and work have been documented by many scholars, beginning with the man himself. When he died, his letter register filled twenty-four volumes. The register's last entry is number 98,721, but this is only a partial count. Charles's letters and photographs are still being discovered, to the delight of scholars and fans.

Charles's own publications, about three hundred separately published items, have been reissued. Prices continue to mount for rare early editions, and other books by and about Lewis Carroll (including this book you are reading) are collectible as well. One collector owns *Alice* books in eighty-one languages!

So many new books and articles have appeared in recent years that it is hard to keep up with all the titles and the theories. One book "proves" that Charles was Jack the Ripper. Another theorizes that he had a love affair with Mrs. Liddell, Alice's mother. Readers can only consider the evidence and decide for themselves what to believe about Lewis Carroll.

Charles's poem *"Solitude"* says:

> I'd give all wealth that years have piled,
> The slow result of Life's decay,
> To be once more a little child
> For one bright summer-day.

As Lewis Carroll, Charles Lutwidge Dodgson created an enduring literary childhood and bright summer days that will never fade so long as people read and enjoy *Alice's Adventures in Wonderland* and *Through the Looking-Glass and What Alice Found There.*

Sources

p. 6   Lewis Carroll, *Alice's Adventures in Wonderland* (New York: Books of Wonder, 1992), 2.

p. 7   Lewis Carroll, *The Lewis Carroll Picture Book*, ed. S. D. Collingwood (London: Collins' Clear-Type Press, [1899]), 261.

p. 8   Ibid., 129.

p. 8   Lewis Carroll, *Alice's Adventures under Ground: A Facsimile of the Original Lewis Carroll Manuscript* (Ann Arbor: University Microfilms, 1964), 90.

p. 9   *Lewis Carroll Picture Book*, 129.

p. 9   *Alice's Adventures under Ground*, 24.

p. 9   *Alice's Adventures in Wonderland*, 29.

p. 10   Caryl Hargreaves, "Alice's Recollections of Carrollian Days As Told to Her Son Caryl Hargreaves," *The Cornhill Magazine*, July 1932, 7.

p. 10   *Lewis Carroll Picture Book*, 261.

p. 10   Stuart Dodgson Collingwood, *The Life and Letters of Lewis Carroll (Rev. C. L. Dodgson)* (New York: Century, 1899), 96.

p. 10   *Lewis Carroll Picture Book*, 261.

p. 14   H. T. Stretton, "More Recollections of Lewis Carroll—II," in Morton N. Cohen, *Lewis Carroll: A Biography* (New York: Knopf, 1995), 290.

p. 15   Collingwood, 13.

p. 16   Lewis Carroll, *The Letters of Lewis Carroll*, 2 vols., ed. Morton N. Cohen (New York: Oxford University Press, 1979), 4.

p. 17   Florence Becker Lennon, *The Life of Lewis Carroll (Victoria Through the Looking Glass)*, 3rd ed. (New York: Dover, 1972), 35.

p. 18   Lewis Carroll, *The Diaries of Lewis Carroll*, 2 vols., ed. Roger Lancelyn Green, (1954; reprint, Westport, CT: Greenwood, 1971), 8.

p. 19   Ibid., 18 (MS: Houghton Library, Harvard University, MS Eng 718.5).

p. 19   Collingwood, 21–22.

p. 20   Ibid., 25.

p. 20   Lewis Carroll, *The Humorous Verse of Lewis Carroll: The Rev. Charles Lutwidge Dodgson* (1933; reprint, New York: Dover, 1960), 7.

p. 21   Collingwood, 30.

p. 22   Ibid.

p. 22   Lewis Carroll, *Lewis Carroll's Diaries: The Private Journals of Charles Lutwidge Dodgson (Lewis Carroll)*, 6 vols. to date, ed. Edward Wakeling (Luton, England: The Lewis Carroll Society Publications Unit, 1993–), 3: 40.

p. 22   Collingwood, 23.

p. 23   Oxford University Statutes, trans. G. R. M. Ward ([Oxford: Oxford University], 1845), 160.

p. 23   Anne Clark, *Lewis Carroll: A Biography* (New York: Schocken, 1979), 64.

p. 23   *Diaries* (Green), 29.

p. 25   Clark, 65.

p. 25   *Diaries* (Green), 28.

pp. 25–26   Matthew Arnold. "Thyrsis," 1866, st. 2, in John Bartlett. *Familiar Quotations*

(Boston: Little, Brown and Company, 1968), 714.

p. 28 C. H. Gibbs-Smith, comp., *The Great Exhibition of 1851: A Commemorative Album* (London: His Majesty's Stationery Office, 1950), 16.

p. 28 Collingwood, 51–52.

pp. 28–29 *Punch,* May 24, 1851, 209.

p. 29 *The Expositor* (1851), in Gibbs-Smith, 32.

p. 30 Collingwood, 53.

p. 30 Ibid., 58.

p. 31 Carroll, *Letters,* 29.

pp. 31–32 Ibid., 31.

p. 32 *Diaries* (Wakeling), 1:88.

p. 32 Collingwood, 60.

p. 32 *Lewis Carroll Picture Book,* 39.

p. 33 Ibid; Ibid.

p. 35 Collingwood, 64.

p. 37 *Diaries* (Wakeling), 2:26.

p. 37 Ibid., 2:42.

p. 38 Ibid., 2:54; Ibid., 2:65.

p. 39 Ibid., 2:78–79.

p. 40 Ibid., 2:119.

p. 40 Carroll, *Letters,* 112–113.

p. 41 Ibid., 3:51.

p. 41 Lewis Carroll, [Review of the 1860 Photographic Exhibition], *Illustrated Times* (January 28, [1860]), in Cohen, 151.

p. 41 *Diaries* (Wakeling), 3:59.

p. 41 Ibid., 3:65–66.

p. 41 Hargreaves, 6.

p. 43 Carroll, *Letters,* 44.

p. 43 *Diaries* (Wakeling), 3:93.

p. 44 Ibid., 3:108.

p. 44 Collingwood, 69.

p. 44 *Diaries* (Wakeling), 3:115.

p. 44 Carroll, *Letters,* 37.

p. 46 Collingwood, 83.

p. 47 Lennon, 79.

p. 47 Carroll, *Letters,* 44.

p. 48 *Alice's Adventures in Wonderland,* 18.

p. 49 *Diaries* (Wakeling), 3:142.

p. 52 *Lewis Carroll Picture Book,* 126–127.

p. 53 Greville MacDonald, *George MacDonald and His Wife* (1924; reprint, New York: Johnson, 1971), 341.

p. 53 *Diaries* (Wakeling), 4:172.

pp. 53–54 Hargreaves, 9.

p. 54 *Diaries* (Wakeling), 4:173.

p. 54 Ibid., 4:214.

pp. 54–55 Ibid., 4:214–215 n. 227.

p. 55 Lorina (Liddell) Skene to Alice (Liddell) Hargreaves, May 1930, (MS: Christ Church), Edward Wakeling, "Two Letters from Lorina to Alice," *Jabberwocky: The Journal of the Lewis Carroll Society,* Autumn 1992, Vol. 21, No. 4, Issue n. 80, 92.

p. 55 Lewis Carroll, *Looking-Glass Letters* (New York: Rizzoli, 1992), 58.

p. 55 Carroll, *Letters,* 63–64.

p. 56 *Diaries* (Wakeling), 4:253 n. 291.

p. 56 Ibid., 4:264; Ibid., 4:267.

p. 57 Ibid., 4:269; Ibid.

p. 57 *Alice's Adventures under Ground,* 1.

p. 58 Ibid., 76.

p. 59 Ibid., 11; Ibid., 15; Ibid., 85.

p. 61 Carroll, *Letters,* 62.

pp. 61–62 *Diaries* (Wakeling), 4:272.

p. 62 Collingwood, 199.

p. 63 Carroll, *Letters,* 65.

p. 64 *Diaries* (Wakeling), 4: 314–315.

p. 64 Ibid., 5:35–36.

p. 65 Ibid., 5:97.

p. 66 Ibid., 5:115.

p. 67 *Alice's Adventures in Wonderland,* 103.

p. 67 Ibid., 143.

p. 67 Carroll, *Letters,* 81 (MS: Berg Collection of English and American Literature,

The New York Public Library, Astor, Lenox and Tilden Foundations).

p. 67   *Diaries* (Wakeling), 5: 131 (MS: Eng 718.5; bMS Eng 718.12 (19)).

pp. 67–68   *The Sunderland Herald*, May 25, 1866, in *Jabberwocky: The Journal of the Lewis Carroll Society* 9, no. 2, (issue no. 42): 38.

p. 68   *Publisher's Circular*, December 8, 1865, in *Jabberwocky: The Journal of the Lewis Carroll Society* 9, no. 1 (issue no. 41): 4.

p. 68   Carroll, *Letters*, 93.

p. 68   Ibid., 94.

p. 68   Collingwood, 130.

p. 69   Ibid., 114–115.

pp. 69–70   Carroll, *Letters*, 106.

p. 70   Collingwood, 120.

p. 70   Ibid., 120.

p. 70   *Diaries* (Wakeling), 5: 371 n. 551.

p. 71   *Diaries* (Green), 270.

p. 71   Ibid., 270.

p. 71   Collingwood, 131–132.

p. 71   Ibid., 131.

p. 71   Clark, 159.

p. 72   Carroll, *Letters*, 123.

p. 72   *Diaries* (Green), 281.

p. 72   Carroll, *Letters*, 146.

p. 73   *Diaries* (Green), 288.

p. 75   Rodney Engen, *Sir John Tenniel: Alice's White Knight* (Aldershot, England: Scholar Press, 1991), 97.

p. 75   Ibid., 93.

p. 75   Collingwood, 148–149.

p. 76   Lewis Carroll, *Through the Looking-Glass and What Alice Found There* (New York: Random House, 1965), 94.

pp. 77–78   Ibid., 132.

p. 78   *Athenaeum*, December 16, 1871, in Cohen, 133.

p. 78   *Globe*, December 15, 1871, in Cohen, 133.

p. 78   Lewis Carroll. The New Belfry [of] Christ Church, Oxford (1872), in *Lewis Carroll Picture Book*, 91.

p. 78   Ibid.

p. 79   Lewis Carroll, *The Vision of the Three T's* (1873) in *Lewis Carroll Picture Book*, 100.

p. 81   Ethel M. Arnold, "Reminiscences of Lewis Carroll," *Atlantic Monthly* [June 1929], in Morton N. Cohen, ed., *Lewis Carroll: Interviews and Recollections* (Iowa City: University of Iowa Press, 1989), 162.

pp. 81–82   Evelyn M. Hatch, introduction to *A Selection from the Letters of Lewis Carroll (The Rev. Charles Lutwidge Dodgson to His Child-Friends)*, by Lewis Carroll, ed. Evelyn M. Hatch (1933; facsimilie, n.p.: Folcroft, 1973), 3.

p. 82   Ibid.

p. 83   *Lewis Carroll Picture Book*, 128.

p. 83   Collingwood, 379.

p. 83   Carroll, *Letters*, 230 n. 1.

pp. 83–84   Collingwood, 380.

p. 84   *Diaries* (Green), 281

p. 85   Henry Holiday, "The Snark's Significance," *The Academy*, January 29, 1898, in Clark, 197.

p. 85   Lewis Carroll, *Lewis Carroll's The Hunting of the Snark* (Los Altos, CA: William Kaufmann, 1981), B [3].

p. 85   Ibid., 100 (MS: Morris L. Parrish Collection of Victorian Novelists,

Manuscripts Division,
Department of Rare Books
and Special Collections,
Princeton University
Library).

p. 85 Ibid., 47.

p. 86 Carroll, *Letters*, 246.

p. 86 Ibid., 254.

p. 87 *Diaries* (Green), 380.

p. 88 Gertrude E. Thomson.
"Lewis Carroll," *The
Gentlewoman,* January 29,
1898, in *Letters*, 347 n. 1.

p. 89 *Diaries* (Wakeling), 5: 244.

p. 89 Carroll, *Letters*, 345–346 n. 2.

p. 89 Ibid., 431; Ibid., 338; Ibid., 619.

p. 90 *Diaries* (Green), 445.

p. 91 Anne Clark, "Lewis Carroll:
The Man and the
Myth"(lecture presented at
the Lewis Carroll Centenary
Programme, sponsored by
the Lewis Carroll Society
and the University of Oxford
Department for Continuing
Education, Oxford, England,
August 21, 1998).

p. 91 *Diaries* (Green), 390.

p. 92 Lewis Carroll. [Manuscript
Diary], 21 September 1880],
in Cohen, 414.

p. 92 *Diaries* (Green), 393.

pp. 92–93 Carroll, *Letters*, 73–74.

p. 93 Ibid., 370; Ibid., 867–868; Ibid.

p. 95 Clark, 253.

p. 95 Carroll, *Letters*, 663.

p. 95 Collingwood, 219.

p. 95 *Diaries* (Green), 412.

p. 96 Lewis Carroll, *The Complete
Illustrated Lewis Carroll*
(Ware, England:
Wordsworth Editions,1998),
1064–1065.

p. 96 Collingwood, 238.

p. 97 Ibid., 237.

p. 98 *Diaries* (Green), 443.

pp. 98–99 Hatch, 6.

p. 99 Collingwood, 259.

p. 99 *Diaries* (Green), 445.

p. 99 Ibid., 448.

p. 101 Carroll, *Letters*, 691.

p. 101 *Diaries* (Green), xx.

p. 101 Carroll, *Letters*, 675.

p. 101 *Diaries* (Green), xxii.

p. 102 Ibid., xxi.

p. 103 Collingwood, 280.

p. 103 Carroll, *Letters*, 812–813.

pp. 103–104 Ibid., 977–978.

p. 104 *Diaries* (Green), xxiii.

p. 105 Ibid., 484.

p. 105 Carroll, *Letters*, 662.

p. 105 Ibid., 870.

p. 106 Caryl Hargreaves, "The
Lewis Carroll That Alice
Recalls," *New York Times
Magazine*, May 1, 1932, 15.

p. 106 Carroll, *Letters*, 822.

p. 106 *Diaries* (Green), 518.

p. 106 *Lewis Carroll: Interviews and
Recollections*, 186.

p. 106 *Diaries* (Green), 537.

pp. 107–108 Carroll, *Letters*, 1155.

p. 108 Collingwood, 330.

p. 108 Ibid., 347–348; Ibid., 364.

pp. 108–109 Gertrude E. Thomson,
"Lewis Carroll," in Clark,
271–272.

p. 111 *Times* (January, 15 1898), in
Derek Hudson, *Lewis
Carroll: an Illustrated
Biography* (New York:
Clarkson N. Potter, 1977), 19.

p. 112 Isa Bowman, *Lewis Carroll
as I Knew Him* (1899;
reprint, New York: Dover,
1972), 3.

p. 116 Words and Music by
GRACE SLICK, © 1966,
1994 IRVING MUSIC, INC.
(BMI), International
Copyright Secured. All
Rights Reserved.

p. 117 Lewis Carroll. "Solitude"
(1853), in *Humorous Verse*, 417.

Selected Bibliography

Titles recommended especially for young readers are marked with an *.

Writings of Lewis Carroll

* *Alice's Adventures in Wonderland.* First published 1865, dated 1866. Reprint, with afterword by Peter Glassman, New York: Books of Wonder, 1992.
* *Alice's Adventures under Ground: A Facsimile of the Original Lewis Carroll Manuscript.* 1864. Facsimile, Ann Arbor: University Microfilms, 1964.

The Diaries of Lewis Carroll. 2 vols., edited and supplemented by Roger Lancelyn Green. 1954. Reprint, Westport, CT: Greenwood Press, 1971.

* *The Humorous Verse of Lewis Carroll: The Rev. Charles Lutwidge Dodgson.* 1933. Reprint, New York: Dover, 1960.
* *The Hunting of the Snark.* 1876. In *Lewis Carroll's The Hunting of the Snark.* Los Altos, CA: William Kaufmann, 1981.

The Letters of Lewis Carroll. 2 vols., edited by Morton N. Cohen with the assistance of Roger Lancelyn Green. New York: Oxford University Press, 1979.

The Lewis Carroll Picture Book. Edited by S. D. Collingwood. London: Collins' Clear-Type Press, [1899].

Lewis Carroll's Diaries: The Private Journals of Charles Lutwidge Dodgson (Lewis Carroll). 6 vols. to date, edited and annotated by Edward Wakeling. Luton, England: The Lewis Carroll Society Publications Unit, 1993– .

* *Looking-Glass Letters.* Selected and introduced by Thomas Hinde. New York: Rizzoli, 1992.
* *The Nursery "Alice."* London: Macmillan, 1889.
* *The Rectory Umbrella and Mischmasch.* 1932. Reprint, New York: Dover, 1971.
* *A Selection from the Letters of Lewis Carroll (The Rev. Charles Lutwidge Dodgson) to His Child-Friends.* Edited by Evelyn M. Hatch. 1933. Facsimile, n.p.: Folcroft, 1973.
* *Through the Looking-Glass and What Alice Found There.* First published in 1871, dated 1872. A Centennial Edition. New York: Random House, 1965.

Resources

* Bjork, Christina. *The Other Alice: The Story of Alice Liddell and Alice in Wonderland*. Stockholm: Raben & Sjogren; New York: Raben & Sjogren, 1993.

* Clark, Anne. *Lewis Carroll: A Biography*. New York: Schocken, 1979.

———. *The Real Alice*. New York: Stein and Day, 1981.

Cohen, Morton N. *Lewis Carroll: A Biography*. New York: Knopf, 1995.

* ———. *Reflections in a Looking Glass: A Centennial Celebration of Lewis Carroll, Photographer*. New York: Aperture, 1998.

———, ed. *Lewis Carroll: Interviews and Recollections*. Iowa City: University of Iowa Press, 1989.

* Collingwood, Stuart Dodgson. *The Life and Letters of Lewis Carroll (Rev. C. L. Dodgson)*. New York: Century, 1899.

* Engen, Rodney. *Sir John Tenniel: Alice's White Knight*. Aldershot, England: Scholar Press, 1991.

* Gardner, Martin. Introduction and notes for *The Annotated Alice: The Definitive Edition*. New York: Norton, 2000.

* Hargreaves, Caryl. "Alice's Recollections of Carrollian Days As Told to Her Son Caryl Hargreaves." *The Cornhill Magazine*, July 1932, 1–12.

* Hudson, Derek. *Lewis Carroll: An Illustrated Biography*. New York: Clarkson N. Potter, 1977.

* Jones, Jo Elwyn, and J. Francis Gladstone. *The Alice Companion: A Guide to Lewis Carroll's Alice Books*. New York: New York University Press, 1998.

Lennon, Florence Becker. *The Life of Lewis Carroll (Victoria Through the Looking Glass)*. 3rd ed., revised and enlarged. New York: Dover, 1972.

Reed, Langford. *The Life of Lewis Carroll*. 1932. Reprint, Folcroft, PA: Folcroft Library Editions, 1974.

* Stoffel, Stephanie Lovett. *Lewis Caroll and Alice*. London: Thames and Hudson, 1997.

* Taylor, Roger, and Edward Wakeling. *Lewis Caroll, Photographer: The Princeton University Library Albums*. Princeton, NJ: Princeton University Press, 2002.

Williams, Sidney Herbert, and Falconer Madan. *The Lewis Carroll Handbook of the Literature of the Rev. C. L. Dodgson*. Edited by Roger Lancelyn Green and Dennis Crutch. Folkstone, England: Dawson, 1979.

Index

Author Acknowledgments

I first thought of this book with my mother and co-author, Jean Shirley. After she died in 1995, I wrote it alone, but with her always in my mind and in my heart.

Thanks to the Lewis Carroll Society and the Lewis Carroll Society of North America for their warm welcomes and considerable assistance. Web sites for these organizations are listed in the bibliography section.

The work of many Carrollian scholars, past and present, formed the basis for this book. Thanks to Anne Clark Amor, Joel Birenbaum, Christina Bjork, Hilda Bohem, Mark Burstein, Sandor Burstein, Morton N. Cohen, Martin Gardner, Selwyn H. Goodacre, August and Clare Imholtz, Karoline Leach, Hughes Lebailly, Charles Lovett, Michael O'Connor, Mark Richards, Sarah Stanfield, Stephanie Lovett Stoffel, Roger Taylor, Alan White, Keith and Liz Wright, and especially to Edward Wakeling.

For support and encouragement, thanks to my husband Richard, daughter Carey, and to these friends and colleagues: Jane and Peter Atkinson, Matt Borrego, Jennifer Crow, Judith Curthoys, Annie Dee, Matt Demakos, Karen Dennison, Monica Edinger, A. and P. M. Fellows, Michael Gorman, Kathy Haug, Marcia Marshall, Janet McMullin, Dee Andy Michel, Marcie Morrison, Denise Sciandra, Joyce Smith, Patricia Walsh Taylor, and especially to Christy Hicks.

Photo Acknowledgments

Cover: Mary Evans Picture Library (top left), © Bettmann/CORBIS (bottom right); Laura Westlund, p. 2; © Mary Evans Picture Library, pp. 6, 7, 9, 11, 13, 21, 24, 25, 26, 36, 37, 39, 42, 48, 49, 51, 60, 61, 63, 66, 73, 74, 75, 77, 80, 81, 91, 94, 101, 104, 111; Angelica Carpenter, pp. 8, 14, 17, 18; *Lewis Carroll: an illustrated biography* by Derek Hudson, New York, 1977, pp. 12 (all), 97; *Punch*, June 17, 1871, p. 29; *The Life and Letters of Lewis Carroll* by Stewart Dodgson Collingwood, London, 1898, p. 40; Collection of Jon A. Linseth, p. 46; Princeton University Library, pp. 34, 45, 52; *Alice's Adventures Under Ground,* by Lewis Carroll, London, 1886, p. 58; © CORBIS, p. 69; © Stapleton Collection/CORBIS, p. 84; Harry Ransom Humanities Research Center, The University of Texas at Austin, p. 87; Courtesy of the Lovett Collection, Winston-Salem, NC, p. 90; © Bettmann/CORBIS, p. 100; Courtesy of All Saints Parish Church, Daresbury, p. 109; AP/Wide World Photos, p. 110; © The Walt Disney Company, p. 115.

All attempts were made to contact the copyright owner. If a photo appears in the book without credit, please contact the Lerner Publishing Group.

127

About the Author

Angelica Shirley Carpenter has written or co-written several award-winning books, including *Frances Hodgson Burnett: Beyond the Secret Garden*, a National Council for Social Studies/Children's Book Council Notable Children's Trade Book in the Field of Social Studies, and *L. Frank Baum: Royal Historian of Oz*, an International Reading Association/ Children's Book Council Children's Choice. She lives in Fresno, California, where she is the founding curator of the Arne Nixon Center for the Study of Children's Literature at California State University and an active member of the Lewis Carroll Society of North America. Her website is <http://zimmer.csufresno.edu/~angelica/>.